The Five Principles of Educator Professionalism

The Five Principles of Educator Professionalism

Rebuilding Trust in Schools

Nason Lollar

ConnectEDD Publishing
Hanover, Pennsylvania

This publication is available at discount pricing when purchased in quantity for educational purposes, promotions, or fundraisers. For inquiries and details, contact the publisher at: info@connecteddpublishing.com

Published by ConnectEDD Publishing LLC
Hanover, PA
www.connecteddpublishing.com

Cover Design: Kheila Casas

The Five Principles of Educator Professionalism. —1st ed. Paperback
ISBN 979-8-9890027-5-7

Praise for *The Five Principles of Educator Professionalism*

As a former teacher, principal, and superintendent, I can attest that Dr. Nason Lollar has captured the heart of building trust in *The Five Principles of Educator Professionalism*. This book can help us all as we strive to increase the level of professionalism in the field of education. It will also be beneficial in retaining teachers, which is a challenge for our entire country at this time. With his recent and relevant experience, Dr. Lollar addresses these topics not just in theory, but from decades of experience.

—Dr. Ben Burnett | President and CEO William Carey University

This book is not just a guide, but a call to action, inspiring educators to embrace their roles with integrity and dedication. By telling our story through the use of real-life scenarios, *The Five Principles of Educator Professionalism* caused me to pause and think about my personal contribution to my school's culture. It is an essential read for anyone seeking to enhance their impact and cultivate a positive, trust-filled school culture.

—Syl Burrell, Ed.D. | Assistant Principal, 2020 Mississippi
Assistant Principal of the Year

If there's ever been a book that should be in the hands of every teacher, *The Five Principles of Educator Professionalism* is the one. No matter if you are a first-year teacher or a twenty-four-year veteran educator, everyone can benefit from the knowledge and wisdom in this book.

—Christy Walker, Ed.S., NBCT | AP Government and Economics
Teacher Germantown High School

Nason Lollar's *The Five Principles for Educator Professionalism* offers invaluable insights for educational leaders nationwide. Drawing from his extensive experience as a principal and leader in education, Dr. Lollar illustrates key principles through real-life scenarios, providing strategies to anticipate and manage challenges. His approach not only emphasizes learning from past incidents but also guides leaders in effective follow-up and knowledge transfer. For educators navigating new leadership roles, this book is an indispensable resource. Highly recommended.

—Ronnie L. McGehee, Ph.D. | Executive Director, Mississippi Association of Secondary School Principals & Mississippi Association of School Administrators

A truly engaging and user-friendly read! Dr. Lollar has effortlessly incorporated practical, real-life scenarios from everyday situations that educators regularly face. From the first chapter, teachers and administrators alike will find themselves deeply engaged and relating to the issues addressed in *The Five Principles of Educator Professionalism*. I even found myself getting misty-eyed while reading the last chapter, as Dr. Lollar's final scenario reminded me of my own experiences, stirring a swell of emotions. This book will inspire you to reflect on your own professionalism and remind you why you chose to be a teacher, an administrator, an educator.

—Dr. David B. Hand | Dean of the Belhaven University School of Education Jackson, MS

The Five Principles of Educator Professionalism is what real educators want to read. Practical wisdom. Applicable and relevant vignettes. Vulnerable insight. An author who is continually learning as well. Truth about growing as a professional that welcomes you to join along as opposed to shouting from behind a podium. This is modern educator professionalism with classic roots.

—Dr. Wesly Bolden | Educator

The Five Principles of Educator Professionalism is a compelling and timely exploration of trust in education. The captivating real-world scenarios engage your intellect and promote introspection. Educators contemplating how they can be a champion of transformation should start with this book. Whether you are a novice or seasoned educator, his practical and straightforward tactics foster professionalism in education. A true grand slam.

—Stephanie Permenter | Director of Student Services, Madison (MS) County Schools

The Five Principles of Educator Professionalism is a must-read for educators who want to enhance their own personal contributions to a culture of learning. It offers a roadmap for fostering integrity, growth, and professional conduct. The book empowers educators to embody professionalism and elevate the educational experience for every student.

—Brent Brownlee | Assistant Principal, Germantown (MS) High School

The Five Principles of Educator Professionalism: Rebuilding Trust in Schools does an exemplary job identifying the foundation for building a strong culture. As Nason Lollar defines professionalism and its variations, he details the importance to ensure success. Dr. Lollar discusses the foundational aspects that are necessary to establishing success for a school community.

—Lewis B. Bradford | Principal, Northwest Rankin (MS) High School

The 5 Principles of Educator Professionalism is an essential read for anyone committed to cultivating integrity, communication, and accountability in today's educational landscape. Nason Lollar masterfully outlines a comprehensive, actionable framework that not only defines professionalism but also provides the tools necessary to rebuild and sustain trust. His insightful analysis and practical guidance make this book an invaluable resource for instructional leaders, educators, and professionals across all fields. A true game-changer in the conversation on professionalism, this book is a must-read for anyone looking to make a meaningful impact in their community.

—Dr. Wesley Quick | Director of High School Services,
Madison County (MS) Schools

In a time of rapid change and increasing skepticism in the world of education, *The Five Principles of Educator Professionalism* provides practical strategies for rebuilding trust in schools. The scenarios in this guide are realistic and thought-provoking, leaving the reader with a fresh perspective on school safety, parent communication, work-life balance, and morale. This is one of the most relevant and accessible professional development books I've read in a while.

—Marie Williams | High School English Teacher

Nason Lollar's use of current, real-world experiences speaks to the heart of school administration today. Establishing and maintaining trust, communication, and morale is recognized and emphasized by Dr. Lollar as the touchstones of effective and meaningful educational leadership. I highly recommend *The 5 Principles of Educator Professionalism* as a genuinely honest and helpful resource for both new and veteran educators alike.

—Ted Poore | Superintendent, Madison County (MS) Schools

The Five Principles of Educator Professionalism stands out for its truthful and honest exploration of the challenges and triumphs faced by educators. Nason Lollar's narrative encourages deep reflection, making it a must-read for both new and tenured educators ready to assume leadership within their schools. His charming storytelling, paired with a solid framework for professionalism, provides relatable and relevant stories that resonate with everyone who serves in a school setting. *The Five Principles of Educator Professionalism* helps educators foster a culture of trust!

    —Heidi Fagerness | Assistant Principal, Chehalis (WA) Middle School 2024 Washington State APOY

In *The Five Principles of Educator Professionalism,* Dr. Nason Lollar shares his innovative approaches and insights on effective teaching practices and professional development. Nason offers a transformative vision for modern education. His comprehensive framework not only addresses the critical issues of trust and professionalism in schools, but also provides actionable strategies for educators to implement. His profound understanding of the challenges facing today's educators, combined with his practical wisdom, makes this book an indispensable resource for teachers, administrators, and policymakers committed to creating a more effective and trusting educational environment.

    —J. Clay Norton, Ed.D. | Belhaven University

The Five Principles of Educator Professionalism speaks to the heart of every teacher and administrator. Each scenario and word of advice is a guide to improving a school's culture. It should be kept at arm's length and used as a reference book, while the bar continues to rise for educators.

    —Anna Thomas | High School History Teacher

Whether you›re seeking personal growth or the next book study, *The Five Principles of Educator Professionalism* should be your next selection. It stepped on my toes and made me laugh, all while forcing me to analyze every aspect of my role as an educator. Dr. Nason Lollar masterfully balances thought-provoking scenarios with real-life experiences to address the challenges that distinguish good educators from great ones. Whether it's your first year or your twentieth, this book should be considered required reading!"

—Jill Knighton | High School Math Teacher

Nason Lollar's *The Five Principles of Educator Professionalism* is a must read for new teachers entering the classroom, experienced teachers wishing to revitalize their career, and administrators looking to strengthen the culture of their school. Educators are faced with so many obstacles, it is easy for an educator to become overwhelmed and lose focus. Because Dr. Lollar has served "in the trenches" as a successful classroom teacher and school administrator, he has seen firsthand the struggles facing our profession today. His keen insight into the field of education has resulted in a must-read book on how to be the best educator you can be.

—Elizabeth Foster | Former Teacher and Director of Human
    Resources, Hinds County (MS) School District

Table of Contents

CHAPTER 1

A Monday Morning

Soggy Cheerios are hard to remove from a sisal rug. That was the first lesson of the day for Coach Daryll Smith. On his hands and knees, removing smushed cereal and warm milk from the ropey grooves. An argument between his younger two children caused the mess. When a large bowl of cereal toppled onto the floor, the argument ended, and the morning routine was suspended.

Workdays usually began at 5:15 a.m. for Coach Smith. That's when he finished his first cup of coffee. Mrs. Smith clocked-in at the hospital by 6:00 each day, so his list to get everyone ready was long. The first task of the day was preparing five breakfasts and four lunches before the sun, or his kids, were up.

This particular Monday started a drug awareness week at school, so dressing the kids to fit the correct theme was a chore. Their 5th grader would cover himself in as much neon yellow as possible, the 3rd grader would be a cowgirl, and the kindergartener would thankfully get to stay in his pajamas.

Their old cowboy hat was too small, though, so the young cowgirl had to have ponytails. Daryll Smith was a 6th grade math teacher and football coach at Southside Middle School, which meant he would tell many people "No" today. His daughter would not be one of them.

The hair style change and spilled cereal pushed their departure back five minutes, raising his heart rate a few extra beats. Accounting for

1

traffic, he would now be at least ten minutes late to school. Daryll's stress level spiked again when he remembered the copier jamming on Friday afternoon. Ready to get home after a long week, he had decided against working late and started his weekend with plans to finish the copying today. He could imagine the line that would be waiting on him in the workroom.

Maybe someone could cover his morning duty post.

As they buckled seat belts, the kids were buzzing about the upcoming day. But Daryll was already dreading his. Between work, practice, and night class, there wasn't a break to be had until EDL 605 dismissed some fourteen hours later. Then he would eat, sleep, and start all over again at 5:15 a.m. Tuesday.

His chest tightened as they pulled out of the driveway. Catching his breath was even hard. He turned on a video for the kids in the back and pulled into traffic.

At work, no one was available to cover the bathrooms. At least, no one that Coach Smith knew. Mrs. Walker across the hall was rushing to a conference, and the teacher next door wasn't in her room. He heard voices farther down the hallway, but heard talk about a concert. Since he didn't know them, he didn't want to interrupt their informal meeting.

Outside of the coaching staff and the teachers close to his room, Coach Smith didn't really know anyone else to ask. Feeling time slip away, he ran down to the workroom.

And the line to make copies was surprisingly short. With the work complete, Coach Smith finally arrived to supervise his assigned bathrooms. He ran a few boys out just before the tardy bell, sent one kid who appeared to be sick to the front office, and headed to class.

～

First block was the high point of the day. The students were prepared for Coach Smith's test on equations. And they jumped into the assignment afterwards as planned. But just after the bell, the day changed.

That's when Wesley Quick, the assistant principal, arrived with an odd request.

"Hey, Coach. Dr. Burrell needs to see you in her office."

He was confused. "Now? I'm about to give a test."

"Yes, 'immediately' was the word she used. Show me the test and I'll get it started for you."

Coach Smith handed over a stack of tests and hurried up the hallway, where he was quickly ushered into the principal's office.

"Have a seat, Coach." Dr. Burrell's office was warm and inviting, but her tone was not. Coach Smith liked his principal and had spent time in this office just last week, when she bragged on his recent benchmark scores. But being here now felt odd. He was supposed to be passing out a test to his 2nd period class.

"Absolutely. How can I help?"

"I received a concerning video from a parent this morning and need to ask you some questions." Dr. Burrell turned her laptop as she spoke and clicked a small triangle at the bottom of the screen.

The monitor showed a cellphone video, with the familiar "Like" and "Share" social media icons on the side. As Dr. Burrell clicked play, Daryll could see a group of boys walking down an empty hallway. He'd never seen the video before, but the kids and the hallway looked oddly familiar.

That's when it dawned on Coach Smith, this was his hallway. Dr. Burrell's office suddenly felt uncomfortable.

The student-videographer followed the crowd from behind, documenting the boasting and profanity of a middle school boy argument. The protests and threats echoed down the empty hallway and burst into the calm of Dr. Burrell's office. She paused the video and zoomed in on two boys who were now standing nose-to-nose in front of the bathroom sink. The remainder of the group formed a large circle around them.

"This video was taken before school and posted online during first block." Dr. Burrell's explanation startled Coach Smith, bringing him back into the conversation.

3

She continued, obviously agitated. "Look at these two boys in the center, Max and Will. I've talked with Max's parents this morning, and they claim Will has been bullying their son in the locker room for the past two weeks. What kind of interactions have you seen between these two boys at football?"

"Nothing, really." Coach Smith replied softly. He looked at the restroom on the computer screen, the same one he was responsible for supervising that morning, and realized he was probably making copies when this video was created. His face felt hot.

"Have you been monitoring the locker rooms like we talked about this summer?" Dr. Burrell asked.

Daryll didn't have a good answer for that question either. "When I can, yes. But there are always kids coming up to me needing equipment fixed. It's hard to be in there all the time."

Dr. Burrell looked back to her computer and clicked play again. Both boys began to swing their arms wildly through the air at each other. After several misses, Will landed solid punches on Max's head and shoulder.

Max countered by stepping back. But as he reached back with his right arm to deliver a blow of his own, he slipped backwards on the tiled floor. Max's head slammed against the sink behind him as he fell.

The impact looked painful on video, but it must've been even worse in person. When Max's head hit the sink, the bathroom—and Dr. Burrell's office—echoed with a loud "CRACK."

The boys jumped in immediately to stop the action. Max was out cold. Will even leaned in with a look of concern.

Eventually, the boys pulled a visibly dazed Max up off the floor. Trying desperately to maintain his composure and his footing, he stumbled out of the restroom as they held him up by the arms.

The final blow for Coach Smith came as Dr. Burrell clicked pause one last time. There he was, frozen in the entrance to the bathroom with a fresh stack of tests under one arm.

Daryll had missed every swing. The fight was over.

The tension in Dr. Burrell's office continued to build, though.

"Coach Smith, Max's father brought this video to us during first block. He arrived here to check Max out from school and take him to the hospital. But before they left, he explained how this video had already been shared dozens of times on social media since classes began today."

"They are currently at the emergency room with Max, who likely sustained a serious concussion from that fall. I hope, for his sake and for yours, that is the extent of his injuries."

Dr. Burrell's next question stung. "Coach, based on my conversation with Max's dad, this scene has apparently repeated itself several times in your locker room this month. You just mentioned that you can't supervise the locker room sometimes. How can we verify if any bullying or fighting is going on, if you aren't there to supervise it?"

Coach Smith could only shake his head. It was hard to speak at this point. The frenzy of his morning, the video of the fight, and the sudden realization that he was partly responsible for Max's injury, was starting to take a toll. He sat there in a daze, thinking back on the morning.

Daryll would give anything to go back and just send a text, or call someone, to make sure his duty post was covered. Maybe he could have prevented all of this from happening.

After an awkward silence, Dr. Burrell's next question hurt even more.

"Coach Smith, your morning duty post is right outside this bathroom. I see you there on the screen with a large stack of papers under your arm. Where were you when this fight took place?"

Before he could answer, the secretary opened Dr. Burrell's door. "Sorry to interrupt, but Dr. Brownlee just called. He asked if you could call his cell as soon as possible."

> "Daryll would give anything to go back in time and make sure his duty post was covered. He could have prevented all this from happening."

5

Dr. Burrell immediately pivoted to her next conversation. "Okay, Coach. That's the superintendent. I need to give him an update. It appears from an email I just received that Max's parents have retained a lawyer. After that call, I will be headed to the hospital to check on Max and discuss the situation with his parents. If you could step over to the conference room now, I just need you to write a statement of events from this morning. You can leave your keys and computer on the conference room table when you finish. At this point, I have no choice but to place you on administrative leave until I'm able to complete the investigation. I will be in touch soon with more details. Please don't discuss this matter with anyone else."

Locating the Breakdowns

Poor guy, right?

If you've spent any time in a school, chances are good that you can sympathize with some part of Daryll Smith's terrible Monday morning. Everyone's schedule is slammed. Everyone is overworked. And every single student on campus has the ability to get themselves into trouble.

Looking back at the difficult conversation between Coach Smith and his principal, it's important to locate the breakdowns that led to this incident.

There were multiple lapses in supervision. By failing to arrive at his assigned duty post on time, Coach Smith provided an environment where a group of boys could get into trouble and get hurt. His choice to prioritize copying a test over school safety was a poor one.

The fight in the bathroom also exposed a supervision issue with the Southside football team. Coach Smith didn't have a good answer for that situation, either. His lack of supervision prevented an accurate statement about potential bullying.

Coach Smith's inability to find a substitute also reveals that he was so disconnected from his colleagues that he could only find one teacher to ask before heading off to the work room.

Any one of these breakdowns could cause major problems, but when they occur in combination with each other, they can hurt students and cause catastrophic damage to a school community.

Assigning Consequences

It's easy to be sympathetic to Coach Smith's plight as he sits in Dr. Burrell's office and realizes the consequences of his actions. He works hard. He's a good teacher and a devoted dad. But Max's parents will not care about any of those attributes while sitting in a hospital waiting room. They have a seriously injured child, and Coach Smith's lapse in supervision created an environment where that injury could occur. The consequences of this incident will be felt for months, if not longer.

Coach Smith's actions on Monday morning will fill all the open spots, and clear off a few others, in his principal's calendar for the foreseeable future. Dr. Burrell will have to find answers as to why this fight happened, what type of bullying was going on in the locker room, and what exactly Coach Smith was doing when those boys decided to stroll into a bathroom and fight.

Investigations of an event like this can disrupt a school all by themselves, even without the fighting and serious injury. After pinpointing each breakdown, Dr. Burrell's next step will be to assign consequences.

We already know the first one, an injured student. That's far and away the worst consequence in this scenario. Direct supervision is a critical part of our responsibility as educators to keep students safe.

Coach Smith is in hot water. He faces even more discipline for his lack of supervision of the bathroom. And the potential bullying at football practice creates a pattern of lapses in supervision. Make no mistake about it, his job is in jeopardy.

Viral videos like the one Dr. Burrell narrated in her office can live online forever. Will and Max will likely be punished again at a later date, possibly years down the road, in the form of awkward questions and treatment from peers and adults when this video inevitably resurfaces. Student fights are bad enough, but when a video of one circulates through the school, it creates an even bigger drag on a school community.

Coach Smith's colleagues will spend days wondering why he isn't at work. They will ask questions around school that will only fuel more speculation about the fight, and his future at the school. *"Is something wrong at home?" "Did they fire Coach?" "I saw him in the car-rider line dropping his kids off at school, but he's not here."* What they won't get are any answers. Confidentiality regarding his standing as an employee will mean that rumors will swirl and keep the conversations going.

An incident like this also impacts the administrators. Usually forgotten in these scenarios, Dr. Burrell is faced with hours of investigating student discipline, and also faces the stomach-turning responsibility of handing out severe discipline to a young employee who works extremely hard to do his job well.

Bottom line, the environment at Southside High School is now a wreck.

Case Studies

If you've spent any time in a grad school class, you're likely familiar with the exercise of analyzing case studies illustrating educator misconduct. But most of those scenarios detail hypothetical incidents you only see once in a blue moon.

I'll admit, wild and crazy events are certainly possible in a school. Analyzing some off-the-wall scenario about a drama teacher who acted out an inappropriate scene with the star football player under a staircase, and whose husband leads a social media campaign to get the principal fired in response to disciplinary action, could happen. Seriously, you can't make up some of these weird situations we see in a school. And there are a ton of different applications to the code of conduct that could apply within a scenario like that. But situations like that are rare.

The scenarios we should be talking about out in the open are the small, daily lapses that can often lead to dramatic consequences within the school community. The fact that we don't talk about getting the daily grind right often enough in teacher preparation programs and professional development is one of the reasons many of us felt unprepared in our first year.

And it wouldn't hurt to throw in a few scenarios that illustrate good examples either. We see wonderful examples of service and collegiality every day. Let's be proactive and promote those stories. The reactive approach to professionalism, like most everything else, is problematic because action after the fact is always too late. The damage is already done at that point.

In the pages that follow, we will use scenarios like this to illustrate the importance for educators to meet the critical requirements of their work consistently. But more importantly, we will see how attending to these requirements in the right manner will prove us to be trustworthy to our students, their parents, and our colleagues.

Professional Conduct and Trust

Professional educator conduct is the hottest topic of conversation in education today. Pick any school in the country, in any community, and conversations about educator conduct dwarf all other topics.

But all that talk about professionalism goes unnoticed, because it always takes place behind a closed door in the aftermath of some incident that has damaged the school community. At that point, everyone just wants to move on as quickly as possible.

We must bring these conversations out into the open. It may be impossible to prevent all breakdowns in professional conduct from occurring in a school, but we must try. That is the goal of this book.

Given the damage these breakdowns in professionalism can cause, an ounce of prevention is worth tons of the cure.

Consider the following chapters preventative medicine. Defining educator professionalism in a meaningful and memorable way will lead us to consume ourselves with the most urgent and important work that should take place in schools every day.

No matter what type of community you serve, the needs of students and parents are always the same: a school staffed by professional educators they can trust. The effort to provide that type of environment always settles into five principles that drive effective educator conduct. When we put *effective teaching and meaningful learning first, remain vigilant to school safety, understand the power of communication, seek balance in our approach to students and colleagues,* and *take ownership of our morale,* great things will happen. Along the way, we will see how our personal attitude and conduct provide the vital "soft skills" we hear so much about. A stronger culture, fortified by the bond of trust among stakeholders in a school community, will be the result.

As our opening scenario so painfully illustrates, it only takes one lapse in professional conduct to cause serious problems in a school community, and erase decades of hard-earned trust.

Why is the process of defining professionalism so important? Because our mission is so important. Because each child's future is too important. And, when you look at it from every angle, it's obvious that lax professional conduct can prevent us from accomplishing that mission.

If we want our schools to improve, our daily professional conduct must first improve. But consistently reaching that high standard is easier said than done.

Just ask Coach Smith.

CHAPTER 2

Defining Educator Professionalism

*B*ack on Coach Smith's hallway, the bell rang to end 1st period. Jill Walker stepped out after the bell and saw Dr. Quick standing in Daryll's doorway.

Something was off.

"Where's Coach?" she asked.

The administrator chose his words carefully. "He...had something come up. I'm filling in until a sub arrives."

Mrs. Walker's day was promising to be a hectic one. If Coach Smith was unavailable, that was puzzling. She'd texted with him this morning about work they planned to do during their planning block. The bell rang and Jill headed back into class and started teaching her students to solve the area of a rectangle.

"Alright, kids! Alright...Can we get started on our bellringer?" This group could be rambunctious at times, but today the buzz was much louder. The kids caught her up to speed quickly. "Miss Walker, did you hear about Max?" Jonathan held up his phone and showed Mrs. Walker the video.

"Wow!" was all she could say. Jill had fortunately missed everything because of a parent conference. The fight looked horrible. And at the end, she could see Daryll standing in the doorway to the bathroom.

That was odd, but there was no time to put all those events together. The remainder of 2nd block was tough. After an hour of pushing students through Geometry problems and redirecting them a hundred times to get back to work and worry about Max later, Jill was worn out.

But she was worried about her friend, too.

The bell to end 2nd block meant lunch. By then, the whole school was talking about the fight. Teachers included. Coach Cox got the ball rolling at the teacher table. "Max's cousin said he might need brain surgery," Then, Coach Combes: "Has anyone heard from Daryll? I swear I saw him in the workroom this morning. He's not answering my texts."

Mrs. Walker's texts had gone unanswered, too. Even though she had missed breakfast, she suddenly wasn't hungry. Jill ran to the workroom to make phone calls to parents about yesterday's test and then one more about Jonathan, whom she suspected had created the video. He had talked about the fight in great detail while completely ignoring his practice problems.

The rumors grew as morning transitioned to afternoon. Down the hall, Mrs. Brister claimed Coach Smith had been fired, possibly for participating in the fight. Mrs. Crissey thought he'd been injured in it.

Everyone was worried about their friend.

But Jill didn't really have time to think. She was scheduled to lead a math department PLC meeting after school, which meant she would spend her planning printing spreadsheets for a data review.

When the fourth text message to Daryll went unanswered, Jill decided to dive into their PD presentation by herself. Being his mentor teacher had been a piece of cake so far. Daryll worked hard and tried the strategies she suggested. Even though he was young, his positive attitude made them fast friends.

Mrs. Walker spent the planning period hastily creating PowerPoint slides to keep her mind off the fight. She had a feeling that her topic for tomorrow, supervision, would be a hot one.

Fourth block presented its usual difficulties. And it didn't help that some of the students had been able to text with Max after lunch. He'd been admitted to the hospital now and had apparently said something to them about suing the school. The buzz grew louder.

When the dismissal bell rang, Mrs. Walker breathed a sigh of relief. She could just focus on her PLC group.

An hour later, Jill tidied up her room and prepared for Tuesday morning. The data meeting had gone well. And the reteaching strategies they discussed fit nicely into her lesson plans for next week, so that was a bonus. But the report from Coach Norton, who'd spoken to Daryll after lunch, was shocking. He was at home on administrative leave and had been instructed not to contact anyone at Southside.

As she considered heading home, Mr. Quick appeared.

"Hi, Jill. I know you and Coach Smith were supposed to share some thoughts on professional conduct and supervision in the PD meeting tomorrow. Could you change directions and add in some points about talking to students who are dealing with bullying? Maybe 10 to 15 minutes, tops. I know you had a student last year who struggled through that. Coach Smith will be out tomorrow. If you could handle that part, Dr. Burrell and I will cover supervision.

The mention of her mentee made Jill sad. "Sure."

Wesley just stood there, looking out the window, obviously stressed. "You know, I wish there was a better way to reinforce professional responsibilities. This fight we had today was terrible, but it could have been prevented...." His thoughts trailed off. A moment later he continued.

"We will discuss it again tomorrow, but covering the basics seems like a lost art. Especially with our younger teachers. When we have a breakdown somewhere, it feels like I haven't done my part to prepare them."

Mrs. Walker grabbed a stack of tests and headed out the door quickly to prevent her emotions from getting the best of her. "Yeah, it does seem like we miss the basics sometimes."

It had been a tough day.

What Is Professionalism?

Choose a random hallway, in any school in America, and it won't take you long to find a classroom that runs like a well-oiled machine. But ask someone how a teacher can serve as "the authority figure in a classroom without being an authoritarian" (Biaggini, 2003, p. 7) and they usually just frown, stare off into space, and look for words that aren't there.

Call it common sense, soft skills, or any other name you like, but words often fail us when we try to describe the actions and attitude required for educators to appropriately work and interact with each other at school.

Years ago, a veteran school board attorney discussed educator conduct at an administrator's conference I attended. By the end of his talk, he had painted himself into the same corner we all find ourselves in when we discuss the topic.

"*What is professionalism?*" he asked the room full of principals, directors, and superintendents. I was struck by the fact that this legal expert, who had spent over thirty years investigating un-professional, and sometimes even criminal, educator misconduct, wasn't being rhetorical. He legitimately wanted an answer.

> "What is professionalism?"

The response, in unison, from a convention hall full of administrators? Crickets.

And after an awkward pause, he couldn't give us a good answer either. The veteran lawyer eventually gave up, joking. "*Defining professionalism is tough. How do you put a concept like that into words? I guess it's kind of like pornography, you just know it when you see it.*"

He made his point. But the answer to this question is so elusive because it typically comes from the eye of the beholder. And in our 21st century, online-all-the-time-society, it's no longer wise to make assumptions. For example, there are teachers out there who've inexplicably combined those two concepts: losing their teaching jobs after being exposed for performing on Onlyfans. If you've never heard of Onlyfans, Google it. You'll understand what they sell when you see it. (Just don't use your district-issued device to do the research, though.)

If that fact wasn't bad enough, there are also scores of people in the comments sections of those stories who defend these misguided educators!

So, yeah, educator professionalism is becoming a lost art. But in a way, the lawyer's description wasn't that far off base. Professionalism is an incredibly difficult concept to describe. But it's not because our work is considered taboo. It's because the work of educating kids and serving families is so complex.

Why Is Professional Conduct Important?

Our first two scenarios show a tale of two teachers. Go back and compare Daryll Smith's and Jill Walker's attributes, and actions, and you would find plenty of similarities. Their to-do lists are exhausting to read, much less accomplish. And, if not for one glaring exception, they both met those requirements well.

The centerpiece of their contracts, just like everyone else's, is a commitment to serve. In today's environment, this one bullet point on the list obligates a teacher to do just about everything in the effort to help children grow and earn a diploma. Millions of teachers across America meet these tasks every day.

How do they do it?

Throughout her day, Mrs. Walker ran through what seemed like an obstacle course to get everything done. She made calls to parents, planned for an upcoming presentation, and led a department data meeting. At the end of the day, she added a duty as designated by the principal before grabbing a stack of papers to grade at home.

Those actions are in addition to the real reason she's at Southside. You know, the actual teaching that took place between the bells. And that doesn't even account for the fact that she completed all these tasks after learning about a trusted colleague's sudden hardship.

These many and varied responsibilities fit together to make "Classroom Teacher" one of the toughest job descriptions in America to fulfill.

The more you think about a teacher's typical day, the more you realize quickly that the list could keep going. The consistency and proficiency we see on a daily basis from these consummate professionals is staggering. They keep their heads down and go to work each day with a commitment to their students and colleagues. They talk the talk and walk the walk. They manage the stress, add on tasks that others can't (or often won't) do, and keep the school on track.

Let's consider some of the more important aspects of the job they must meet each day:

Content: Whether it's reading skills or calculating angle measures, teachers who excel at their craft get the content right. They discuss their lessons in the hallway with colleagues and badger their principal for permission to see that sought-after trainer across the country. Content expertise is a priority.

Learning Environment: But love of content doesn't supersede their understanding of pedagogy. There is always an order to their chaos. Every day of the school year, they meet the appropriate safety requirements to protect their students and colleagues, and balance that with appropriate engagement.

Accommodations: And they know every single one of their students. Strengths and weaknesses are understood early. Every kid, in every seat, has a story and these pros want to learn it. With that knowledge secured, they build relevance into their lessons.

High Expectations: Good teachers understand enough about the rigors of the world outside their classroom to push kids. Instead of wasting time trying to smooth out the road, they prepare students for adversity.

Assessment: Great teachers assess as much as they instruct, in order to accurately gauge student learning and adjust as needed.

Relationships: And they can explain a poor grade to little Janie's parents because they've already built a relationship on the front end with the student and the parent.

Not bad for a day's work, huh? And most everyone finds a way to exceed these professional expectations while also denying themselves a trip to the bathroom for hours at a time, or enduring the state fair-like spectacle of choking down a lunch in five minutes while supervising a cafeteria full of children.

The Bar Keeps Rising

But the bar educators must meet to adequately educate students continues to rise. The current technological revolution we are experiencing is a good example of how a changing society can impact the work of an educator. The changes associated with cell phones and social media make it easy (for most people) to sympathize with the work of teaching, because these innovations have reorganized the way school is conducted. And in many cases, they've made the job harder.

In our haste to create more connection between people, our technological society has opened a daunting new Pandora's box. The introduction of these cutting-edge technologies in the early 2010s unleashed an earthquake across school campuses that is still shaking education to its core. Smart phones, able to surpass the computing power of early space vehicles, now serve as a high-tech method for inattentive students to bypass the learning process. Considering this shift, it's easy to see why the pendulum is beginning to swing back against the presence of these devices at school.

And even though we are inundated with this distance-shrinking technology, we instead use them to separate ourselves. In one of the more confusing sociological consequences of constant smartphone use, constant communication by text and video has chilled personal interaction. We now connect too much online, but are hesitant to engage in face-to-face conversation. Our students' mental health, not to mention our own, has suffered dearly as a consequence.

Thanks to this technologically-induced silence, small disagreements fester, becoming larger issues. The effect on our students is hard to understand, but obvious to anyone who works in a school. It's not uncommon for educators to field complaints from students about a mean classmate who wants to fight.

Their offense? *"She looked at me."*

Seriously?

All this "progress" combines to create a social environment that feeds off conflict. And while the job grows more difficult, the challenge has compounded because many schools now face a shortage of qualified teachers.

Most states have addressed these shortages by creating pathways to ease the way for industry professionals to earn a teaching license. There were already plenty of odd combinations within any given faculty. But now it's possible to see a first-year teacher, fresh out of a school of education, beginning their career on the same hallway as a former engineer, a military retiree, and a biology major who is waiting to enter medical school (NCES, 2018).

Each of these individuals own a wealth of knowledge and life experience to share with students. More importantly, they share a desire to serve. But they also bring old work expectations to their new teaching job. School districts should be able to welcome these professionals into their buildings and help them enjoy a smooth transition.

This new variance in the educator workforce, combined with large generation gaps, and the immense changes introduced with each new generation of teachers, adds a new professional development responsibility to school districts and highlights the need for a renewed focus on professional conduct.

In an age when most people depend on the algorithm of their social media feed for reading material, school districts would be wise to go farther than simply handing new teachers a staff handbook, patting them on the back, and sending them off to work with three staff development days to prepare for an entire school year.

We must get everyone in a room together and spell out the requirements for meeting all these crucial needs and sustain that process over the long haul. That's the challenge of attempting to define educator professionalism.

Professionalism and School Culture

So, what are school leaders to do when confronted by challenges that would make professionals in other career fields run for cover? In the face of this laundry-list of tasks, true school leaders do what they do best. They lead.

These servant leaders roll up their sleeves and get down to solving problems. They welcome the renewed focus on accountability that communities demand. They take the first step in creating a positive environment for students to learn and adults to work. They understand the importance of a strong school culture and they go to work happy to play their role in it. They come to work every day with the goal of responding to society by ignoring the noise and taking responsibility for the one thing they can actually control: Themselves.

Good teachers improve culture. But school leaders apply this axiom in both directions. Good cultures can improve teachers, too. The old cliché of a rising tide lifting all boats exists for a reason. And if you have any experience in a school building, you need not scour through volumes of research to know this.

But even though there are libraries full of books encouraging educators to build strong cultures, invest in their teachers, and see those teachers invest in students, people still go to work every day in toxic school environments. Educators who work in these weak cultures often throw up their hands in disgust, wondering what to do about the most recent frustration. These people complain about their work environment in the same way Mark Twain described the weather; constantly complaining about their culture, but never doing anything about it.

So, how can school leaders help their colleagues improve school culture? Well, it would probably help if we could simplify the idea of culture down to the specific actions an educator can take to affect culture. Handing over five pages of open-ended job responsibilities hasn't exactly served as a good teacher recruitment, or school improvement strategy.

Teachers, administrators, and support staff who come to work each day with a positive attitude and a desire to do their part in building a healthy school environment are the building blocks of trust within a strong school culture. And these rock stars who turn in such good work on a consistent basis aren't guessing when it comes to doing the right thing for their students and colleagues.

Often ignored in those legal talks is an explanation of how one person's impact on a school culture is immense and serves as the first step an individual can take in playing a personal role in their school's improvement. Putting these two concepts together, we can define educator professionalism in terms of a person's effect on the big picture: *Educator professionalism is an individual's personal contribution to a culture of learning.*

> Educator professionalism: an individual's personal contribution to a culture of learning.

20

Chances are good you've recently heard someone speak the phrase, "Everyone is a leader." When people use this phrase, they are really speaking to the importance of personal conduct at work. But it might be more appropriate to describe ourselves as "builders" when you consider the importance of school culture. Hopefully, you are spending your time on construction, instead of demolition, when it comes to contributing to the culture of learning at your school.

By looking at our daily personal actions and attitude, which role do we play? We should constantly be asking ourselves, "*What am I doing to elevate the culture of learning at my school?*"

If we view our work in this light, defining professional conduct is no longer an indefinable concept, but instead a list of priorities that express our dedication to the school community.

Professionalism then becomes a personal mission statement that prompts us to reflect.

What am I doing that strengthens the culture at my school?

What am I doing that weakens it?

As we consider these two important questions, five principles rise to the top of this exhaustive job description constituting one of the most complex concepts in the world of work: Educator professionalism

CHAPTER 3

Rebuilding Trust

"**M**RS. HARRISON, THERE IS A PARENT IN THE FRONT OFFICE TO SEE YOU." *Amanda Harrison's radio loudly interrupted the conclusion of an Algebra I data meeting. She checked a text from the secretary as she began the long walk up to the office:*

> "William Ware's parents are in the attendance office demanding to see you. They are MAD but won't talk to anyone but you!"

"Oh, boy. Here we go again." Amanda thought.

Mrs. Harrison responded with a quick "10-4" and considered her difficult relationship with the Ware family as she started up the long hallway. To say she knew them well would be an understatement. Will Ware had been the class clown in her 8th grade Civics class last year, receiving more discipline referrals than any student she'd ever taught.

But this year, they'd moved up to high school together. Will was now a freshman, and Mrs. Harrison was now a first-year assistant principal over 9th graders. With one week to go before the Thanksgiving holidays, this year had been just as tough.

23

Amanda's thoughts immediately went to Will's big incident months ear-lier when Officer Garcia, the school resource officer, was alerted to some sus-picious behavior in the boy's bathroom. When he quietly strolled in behind a group of boys, Will was standing in the center of the group, his head engulfed in a cloud of white mist.

When Amanda found them in the office, Will was seated across the conference room table from Officer Garcia. Three brightly colored vapes lay between them. If the situation wasn't bad enough at that point, Mr. and Mrs. Ware arrived shortly after and immediately went to Level Ten with their protests.

"WHY IS OUR SON IN THE FRONT OFFICE? THIS IS RIDICULOUS! HOW DO YOU KNOW THESE THINGS EVEN BELONG TO HIM?" Mrs. Ware's frantic voice echoed around the con-ference room.

Amanda tried to remain calm and explain the situation as she knew it, although details were still cloudy in her own mind. "Mrs. Ware, Offi-cer Garcia entered the boy's restroom because a teacher overheard the boys talking in the hall and they mentioned 'smoking' in their conversation. When he entered the bathroom, three boys were standing around a cloud of smoke. Will was in the middle, holding one of these vapes."

Officer Garcia picked up the description at that point. "When we arrived at the office, I asked Will if he had anything else in his pockets. He removed two more vapes from his left front pants pocket." Garcia pointed at the electronic cigarettes on the table as he spoke.

Mr. Ware jumped in. "YOU ARE HARRASSING MY CHILD! AND WHAT ABOUT THE OTHER TWO BOYS? DID YOU INTERROGATE THEM LIKE THIS? WE HAVE HAD ENOUGH. YOU PEOPLE SHOULD KNOW BETTER. I SWEAR, BRINGING LAW ENFORCEMENT INTO A SITUATION LIKE THIS IS THE ABSOLUTE WORST WAY TO DEAL WITH A CHILD!"

Mr. Ware had pointed at Will as he finished his complaint, which the young man evidently took as a cue to air his own grievances. "YEAH, THAT POLICEMAN FOLLOWS ME AROUND ALL THE TIME. HE'S OUT TO GET ME!"

Amanda knew she needed to respond to that comment. It was obvious that Officer Garcia was straining to withhold a loud reaction of his own. She tried to ignore Will's tone of voice and attempted to steer the conversation back to the facts. "Officer Garcia was called to that bathroom based on a teacher's report ---"

The 9th grader rudely cut her off, preventing her from bringing up anything else. "JUST GO AHEAD AND EXPEL ME! THIS SCHOOL IS SUCH A JOKE. JUST EXPEL ME NOW AND BE DONE WITH IT. YOU'RE GOING TO DO WHATEVER YOU WANT, ANYWAY. YOU ALWAYS HAVE."

Feeling some momentum, he threw in one more jab for good measure.

"YOU DON'T CARE ABOUT ME!"

"YOU DON'T CARE ABOUT ME!"

For the first time in the conference, the room fell silent. Mrs. Harrison, reeling inside from this eye-opening initiation into school administration, tried mightily to remain calm. But that last comment struck a nerve.

Amanda knew that, as an administrator, she was subject to some ill-will from parents and students, but to hear William Ware—a kid that she bent over backward accommodating in her classroom last year—claim that she didn't care about him was the last straw.

She looked Mr. Ware in the eye, and then his wife. Finally, her eyes settled in on Will.

"Look, Will, I understand you're frustrated. I am, too. And I know that there are many things that infuriate you right now because discipline consequences will be the next thing we talk about. But I'm here, willing to do

whatever I can to help you. We have rules here about vapes because they are unsafe for students. You knew that, but you violated it anyway."

"Now, you can say whatever you want to about this situation, but you can't say that I don't care. I assure you, there are a hundred different places I'd rather be right now than participating in a shouting match about vapes, but I'm still here. I've spent twenty years working in schools to help students and I'm here now, dedicated to helping you through this situation, too."

Amanda sat back, finished. She wasn't sure how that would be received, but she had at least felt better. The Ware's stared back, speechless. Amanda would never forget that conference.

But she hadn't spoken with them since that day. As she opened the door to the attendance office, she braced for impact with two irate parents.

Mrs. Ware was trying to compose herself when Amanda walked into the attendance office. Mr. Ware looked sick, staring off into space. Will paced around the small office in front of his parents, red-faced and looking like he was about to lose it, too. Amanda was instead dealing with a distraught family.

"Good morning. How can I help today?" Given their appearance, that was all she could think to say as they walked back to the conference room. Everyone took the same seats as their last meeting, when they had railed at Amanda and defended their son's poor decisions.

But today was different. Mrs. Ware described the situation. "Mrs. Harrison, Will didn't go to class today because he has been threatened by another student. The profile that created the posts is a made-up name, so we don't know who it is. Will received the texts last night about fighting at school. I've never seen such hateful messages from a kid. Several other boys posted a live conversation overnight making similar threats. They even talked about guns!"

Mr. Ware picked up the story here. "Apparently, they are mad about Will becoming friends with a girl in his algebra class. This could be someone that sits beside him in class. We don't know what to do next."

26

Before Mrs. Harrison could respond, Will spoke quietly, his lip quivering. "My mom and dad wanted to go to the police department this morning, Mrs. Harrison. But I'm scared that will only make it worse. What do you think we should do? I don't know who else to trust."

Mr. Ware pleaded for an answer. "Yes. Mrs. Harrison, what should we do?"

Mrs. Ware leaned forward and stared at Amanda through tears, unable to speak.

Now, it was Amanda's turn to be speechless.

Her only thought, as she tried to assemble a response, was, "It took two years, but they finally trust me."

The Foundation of a School Community

Professionalism might be a hard word to define, but trust is an easy one. To date, I've found no less than eighteen different definitions for it. And just about all of them apply well in a school setting. While you probably won't find the word "trust" in your contract, conducting ourselves in such a way that parents see us as trustworthy is exactly the work we should be doing.

We went to great lengths to spell out the highlights (and, admittedly, some low points) of educators' to-do lists in Chapter Two. And we also looked at how those rock stars meet the requirements on a daily basis. But we really haven't discussed the hardest part. Usually unspoken in this exhaustive job description is the open-ended legal responsibility that serves as the foundation of America's educational system.

Serving *in loco parentis*, the Latin phrase that translates literally to "in place of the parent," is the legal responsibility teachers shoulder every day at work. If you aren't familiar with the term, take a moment to contemplate the weight behind those three little Latin words. Standing *in loco parentis* means agreeing to stand in as a parent for every kid on campus. For most teachers, that means substituting for mom or dad for about one-hundred-and-fifty students, from one-hundred-fifty different homes, with one-hundred-fifty different sets of expectations, for one-hundred-eighty days.

Given the styles of parenting we see today, that also translates into about one-hundred-fifty combinations of good, bad, or ugly home situations. Considering the job in this light, it's easy to see why serving as an educator can pull a person in different directions.

Another way to describe the *in loco parentis* principle is that it places educators into a position of trust over young people while they attend school. When students and parents join into a school community, it's because they see us as worthy of that trust.

This foundational trust is illustrated each fall, as droves of tearful parents clog the driveways and parking lots of the local kindergarten. The first day of school is an unforgettable rite of passage for parents. That's because the bond between parent and child, and the inevitable separation that happens on the first day of school, creates a life-changing fear in the heart of every parent.

Forget the curriculum, the lunch menu, or how nice the bulletin boards look. In that moment, parents have only one question rotating through their minds: *"Can I trust you to keep my kid safe?"*

If you've seen current attendance rates, or the educational options that are now available outside of compulsory public school attendance laws, we should operate with an understanding that this trust is not to be assumed.

Communicating the importance of this fragile trust should now be considered a necessity for school improvement as well. And why should it move up everyone's priority lists? Because even the smallest missteps can violate that trust and halt the good work of every other employee in a school district in its tracks. If we're hammering out a definition for professionalism, we must see trust as its foundation.

While the challenges to building that trust are well-documented, it's also important to understand the context of the times in which we live. We just encountered the greatest disruption to American life since September 11, 2001. As we happily left school on March 6, 2020, we had no idea that Spring Break would last several months. Within a week, every avenue of American society closed indefinitely as a response to the threat of Covid-19.

We will be dealing with the effects of this disruption for the foreseeable future.

~

Completing the 2019-2020 school year after the shutdown was bizarre. Looking back at the experience of conducting school during the pandemic shows a microcosm of American life for those two fateful years.

At our school, we spent most of our time as administrators in the Spring of 2020 guarding 200,000 square feet of empty space, and transitioning in-person school to Teams and Zoom. District technology teams performed yeoman's work to manage the new volume of traffic, while district staff figured out a way to credit teachers for time worked at home. And teachers, for their part, took a crash course on becoming online instructors. And documenting students' physical attendance through a virtual platform? Yeah, like I said, it was tough.

A month later, small groups of people were allowed onto campus. As a process for completion of the school year was finalized, we did our best to create something special for a class that lost the end of their senior year. The result was the longest graduation ceremony ever.

At our school, parents were instructed to drop their graduates off at a side entrance, then drive around to enter by the cafetorium. Outside (properly distanced and masked, of course) they would wait for their appointed graduation time. When their turn came, the family entered our cafetorium and experienced an individual commencement ceremony. The principal and superintendent would welcome them on the stage for a picture. Then we would usher in the next graduate with their family.

A Class of 2020 spacing sign from our school. These signs marked the appropriate space for families to stand, properly distanced from other groups, as they awaited their graduate's individual ceremony.

We used to pride ourselves on conducting a graduation in one hour. The commencement ceremony of 2020 took us a week. Eight hours of individual ceremonies for four days is how long it took us to send 250 seniors out into the world that year.

We spent that summer learning about virus mitigation and hiring new staff. We learned how to interview online. As we narrowed down our lists of candidates, we would bring them in for a "face-to-face" interview. But face-to-face isn't really accurate, because we had to conduct the interview masked, in a classroom with desks spread so far apart it seemed like we were playing a weird Halloween version of four corners.

We would hire teachers, set them up with a mentor, assign them a classroom and rosters of students, and couldn't even recognize them with their mask off. Then, reopening in-person school in the fall semester of 2020 is even harder to explain.

We approached that school year longing for the return of our dearly missed students, but hesitant to deal with the virus. When classes finally resumed, our administrative team transitioned into a new duty, contact tracer for a campus containing 1,500 people. Staring at seating charts, measuring the distance between desks, consulting quarantine timelines, tracking down subs, covering classes, creating shower-curtain barriers around vulnerable teachers' desks and spraying aerosol disinfectant in rooms where someone had displayed symptoms were our new daily tasks.

Mitigating the risk of Covid-19 was a hopeless task. And by late fall of 2020, our frustration began to grow. We were unsure of the effectiveness of these measures at first. But anything we could do that would allow school to continue was seen as worthwhile.

But the harder we worked, the longer the absentee list grew. I'll never forget the most sobering statistic of the pandemic, which illustrates the infamous "Covid Gap." At my school, we quarantined OVER TWO HUNDRED STUDENTS for ten days or more during the 2020-2021 school year. And a large number of those mandatory absences were kids who never got sick. These "close contacts" had to complete a quarantine period that functioned more like a vacation.

The one task that dwarfed all those added work commitments for us contact tracers was talking to parents on the phone. For a year-and-a-half, we battled Covid and served as a sounding board for our community. The sentiment was unanimous. Phone call after phone call revealed our community's frustration. With everything.

It wasn't my place to offer an opinion, but I couldn't blame them for feeling that way. There was sickness, death, job loss, economic strain, and uncertainty in every phase of life. The frustration was so strong across the country, you could feel it. Frustration with illness and a lack of faith in our government's approach to the illness (and to just about everything else). That frustration grew as protests erupted; political upheaval spilled onto the streets. The result? Faith in public education waned.

And through it all, our team spent hour after hour in our offices on the phone. That frustration traveled through the line clearly. And we were lucky. Most of our phone calls ended with a, "Thank you for your support."

But there were definitely some complaints. It wasn't out of the norm in those days to field a phone call from parents who felt our school was being too strict with Covid guidelines, and within an hour field a call complaining because we weren't enthusiastic enough in our efforts to mitigate the virus.

Sometimes, I feel that educators who endured the pandemic from the front lines, confronting these issues daily, deserve a special designation. The years 2020 and 2021 really mean something extra when you see them on a resume.

This immediate, wholesale change of American schools and public society, repeated across all public institutions and fruitless in the eyes of so many Americans, served to further erode a century of hard-earned trust. As the pandemic ended, and life opened back up, this trust didn't magically reappear.

It was a crazy time. An era that we all hope will stay in the past. But when we consider the state of education today, with its growing challenges, changes, and responsibilities, it's important to realize how the erosion of public trust in all public institutions through Covid, or the social media craze, or whatever it is that put the last decade on steroids, all served to harm our mission.

The Covid-19 pandemic, and its effect on American culture cannot be ignored. We must understand how that period damaged public trust and own up to our role in it, if we are ever going to push the reset button and rebuild that trust.

Our Greatest Challenges

Most of the school-level issues that arose from the pandemic were already there. Covid-19 just amplified them.

Does a child really need to be at school to learn? Chronic absenteeism, a constant pre-pandemic problem, still hasn't recovered. Evidently, parents are still grappling with the answer to that question. We need to be able to make the case for students to return to classrooms. Have we reflected on our impact on this pervasive apathy toward school attendance?

Mental health, an issue that skyrocketed with the expanded reach of technology and social media, became an even bigger issue for students, parents, and teachers. Wonder why? Well, internet use exploded during the pandemic, too. Have we equipped students to navigate the dangers of online use? Well, screen time during the school day, *on school-issued devices*, hasn't slowed either. The public needs to know that we are serious about helping students overcome the constant need to be online, and provide them with a safe online environment.

Discipline issues, and sometimes discipline policies, were exposed as well. Kids that participated in the "devious licks" challenge weren't making a passive-aggressive statement that school bathrooms needed remodeling. As we helped custodians pull pencils out of toilet drains and replaced bathroom mirrors, it was obvious there was a disconnect in the relationship between educators and students.

Political unrest became the norm. Forget the old days where we debated and fought over differences of opinion. Thanks to our always-online, argue-every-point culture, we can't even agree on facts. Do we have a plan to teach proper interaction and debate?

These factors affected the public's trust in EVERY institution. And no school, regardless of how successful before the pandemic, was immune. But in addition to the societal factors from the outside, there are factors present within as well.

We are human. We make mistakes. And the inevitable breakdowns in professionalism that every school experiences always seem to occur at precisely the wrong time. In an age where our margin for error is shrinking, we must minimize these unforced errors that further erode trust.

The violation could be as simple as a dig to get the last word in at the end of a parent phone call, or as big as teacher misconduct that leads to an arrest. But breakdowns in professionalism can undo a school community in a heartbeat.

Serving as a school administrator during the pandemic, seeing the amplification of these issues up close, made it clear to me that solving them and rebuilding trust in our schools will be the greatest challenge of our careers.

But in watching so many outstanding educators catch their breath, dry their tears, overcome this convergence of challenges, and go back into that last period class, I realized that this is the challenge for which we were called. Like it or not, if you are serving in a school right now, you were called specifically to serve in this moment.

Thankfully, there is still a great deal of common ground in America. Don't let the distractions, obstacles, and media influencers fool you. There are so many shared priorities in every community across America right now it's unbelievable. In fact, one of them is right there in our fictional, but highly possible, opening scenario. Did you catch it?

When Max's head hit the sink, the bathroom—and Dr. Burrell's office—echoed with a loud "CRACK." The boys jumped in immediately to stop the action. Max was out cold. Will even leaned in with a look of concern.

Those of us who work in a school building with kids know this kind of incident can certainly happen, supervised or not. You've been in those bathrooms. But even in such an unfortunate situation, even in a middle school boy's bathroom, you can still catch a hint of the importance of school safety—a bedrock component of school community trust—that must exist in a school. Kids understand it, and even if they won't admit it, they want it, too.

This belief system, based on trust, is surprisingly consistent across America. Go to an urban environment like New York City, the rural silence of Camden, Mississippi, or pick out the nicest, newest suburban school in the heart of Texas. Schools in America live and die by the bond of trust that is shared between the educators, students, parents, and the school community.

It's the most fragile element in a relationship, but trust is built by people who unselfishly serve others' best interests. That principle travels across all school district lines. Regardless of the population. Through daily discipline, we will slowly earn back that trust.

Building Trust

That surprising vote of confidence at the end of our third scenario illustrates the way forward for educators who want the best for their school communities. Mrs. Harrison, in all her frustration with a difficult disciplinary relationship, verbalized one of the essential tenets of the foundational trust we so desperately seek. Regardless of how difficult the situation is, we are here to do what's best for our students. When we verbalize that commitment, and demonstrate it over the long haul, the payoff is huge.

By taking advantage of a teachable moment with the Ware family, Mrs. Harrison tapped into a valuable principle of strong relationships, and framed it in terms of her purpose. How was that for an impromptu speech fueled by frustration? Pretty impressive professionalism, along with a Herculean show of self-discipline, when you think about it.

We talk about relationships all the time, but this scenario shows an important aspect of educator-student relationships that can often be missed. Jimmy Casas, in his book *Culturize* (2017), stated the principle in this way:

> [We must] allow the students to get to know us. I don't mean get to know us only in terms of our personal lives. I mean that we invite them in to see our core. What drives us to do what we do? What gets us up in the morning and pushes us to want to teach? From what do we draw to make our decisions? It is imperative that our students know our core principles, so they know what to expect. (Casas, 2017, p. 27)

Spending time and effort at odds with students and parents can be one of the most frustrating aspects of the job. But persevering through those incidents, while maintaining a proper focus, can yield some of the strongest bonds. Heated and stressful discipline conversations, while admittedly uncomfortable, can be some of the most important moments in a student's life. That's why the troublemakers often become the ones you bond with most closely. After the struggles, they saw you stick it out. The result? They trust you.

Common ground between schools, parents, and the community is centered around what's best for children. There may be some discussion, disagreement even, on issues around the edges. But doing our part to support a positive culture of learning is how we meet parents and the community on an even footing. It is important to verbalize to students and parents our core values.

Need help spelling out those core principles? Let's drill down into the true foundation of a successful school. What's the most important work we can consume ourselves with every day? What is the most urgent need for our students right now?

Well, answering those questions is how we rebuild, or strengthen, that trust. Paying them lip-service won't do any good. It takes action. Doing what's best for students rebuilds trust. Take those actions and put them on the wall. That's professional conduct.

Five principles, common to every school, student, parent, and community in America, must be weaved so tightly throughout our to-do lists that our daily conduct shows stakeholders who we are and just how committed we are to serving them. They can't just be *what we do*, they must be *who we are*.

These five principles form an easy to remember framework that keeps us on track, focused on the most important parts of our job. When we are consumed with accomplishing each of these five principles each day, we are certain to build TRUST within our school community.

Teaching and learning come first.

Remain vigilant to threats.

Understand the power of communication.

Seek balance.

Take ownership of our morale.

Teaching and learning must come first.

Whether you occupy an office, a classroom, or the roads between schools and district office, true professionals know how to stay focused on the main thing. Supporting teaching and learning means everyone has an instructional leadership role.

And when everyone sees themselves as an instructional leader, collaboration and professional development are just as important as student learning. Good teachers model good learning. They also model reflection and understand that school improvement starts with them.

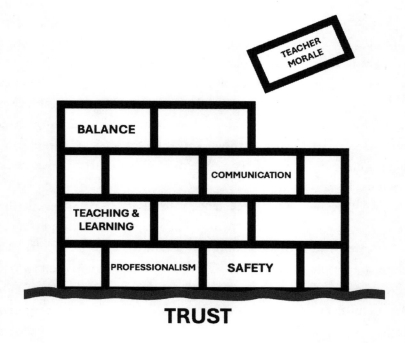

Through the proper use of data and assessment, professionals who prioritize learning don't just make an effort towards equity, they achieve it. School communities trust teachers that commit to learning with every fiber of their being.

Remaining vigilant to safety.

From nightmare lockdown scenarios, and the scourge of intimidation, to educators who abuse their position to take advantage of children, educators who are dedicated to a safe campus understand that no one is immune to danger. Dedication to keeping all students safe and ready to learn is another bedrock component of professionalism.

Educators who remain vigilant understand the nonnegotiable actions that no one in a school community can compromise. And when there are responsibilities that compete for their time, they never allow a trade-off to occur that can shortchange student safety.

In schools that value vigilance regarding safety, mandatory reporting is one of the most important responsibilities of the job. Whether it's as harmless as entering grades regularly so parents can check their child's progress, or a report to authorities to protect a student's safety, professionals forget their personal beliefs about the dangerous times we live in and embrace their role as protector. Safeguarding the school environment is everything to these professionals.

Understand the power of communication.

This is how we do the work of educating. If those first two tasks weren't enough, communication might be even more important. Official communication that documents the work we do, unofficial communication that expresses our attitude, and a dedication to listening well, combines to make our interactions invaluable to the success of our schools.

If you boil down the work in that exhaustive job description to its simplest terms, what educators really do every day is talk to people. Professional educators, adept at the art of interacting with people on a massive scale, understand the power of their words and also understand the power of every single interaction.

Seek balance to stay healthy.

Educators who learn to manage change, and work to mitigate it, are usually the best equipped to deal with the rigors of the job. Striking a balance in our interactions, our attitude, and how we treat ourselves can be the difference maker that turns a good year into a good career.

Self-care, a concept often distorted by the indulgence gurus and self-proclaimed influencers, means resting, recharging, and then reconnecting.

Striking just the right tone in situations for which a protocol does not exist means staying connected with supportive colleagues and learning from experience. That's how we take care of ourselves so that we can continue to serve students.

Take ownership of your morale.

Teachers who know how to safeguard their morale take personal responsibility for the climate of a school. Negativity isn't entertained, indifference isn't allowed, and helplessness is prevented.

Educators who understand professional responsibility protect their morale because it's our most direct personal impact on school culture. When we own our morale, and work to keep it positive, we do our part to improve school culture in even the darkest climates.

~

When our daily walk aligns with these five principles, good things happen. When educators are consumed by a commitment to these principles, they are less likely to commit unforced errors that can harm kids, end careers, and damage the school community.

By dedicating ourselves to these five principles we will rebuild the trust that our school communities so desperately crave.

The TRUST framework spells out the basics that are common to the custodian, the bus driver, the teacher, and the superintendent. The half-life of that toxic environment is only the length of time it takes to make a commitment to rebuilding trust with your students, their parents, and your colleagues.

Parents who see these five behaviors repeated throughout the school year would be proud to have these professionals stand in their place as a guardian for their kids' growth and development.

Now, let's start building TRUST.

CHAPTER 4

Teaching and Learning

Hi, Anna,

    I'm sure you've heard by now…we are moving to a block sched-ule next year. I need to put a team together to help our teachers prepare for this change and could really use your experience to help with the transition. Could you attend a meeting tomorrow after-noon to discuss implementation?

    Thanks,

    Elizabeth

*I*t had been two months since that message landed in Anna's inbox. Maybe it was weakness, maybe it was the pleasant thought of recon-necting with a former neighbor on her hallway, or maybe she was just tired at the end of a long day; but Anna had quickly agreed to participate.

That agreement joined her with fifteen other teachers who met regularly to prepare for an upcoming district-wide professional development day. Their task was a big one, presenting best practices to their colleagues and assisting their district's transition to a full block schedule.

The work sessions had gone well. Elizabeth had assembled a good team, trained them well on different aspects of planning for a block schedule, and listened to the group's concerns as they adjusted the agenda.

But as Anna stood at the front of her school's cafeteria, nervously await-
ing her turn to speak to 150 teachers, she wished she had just replied to
Elizabeth's email with a one-word answer:

NO.

Anna's first-ever assignment as a Professional Development Pre-
senter would be discussing the importance of breaking lesson plans for a
90-minute class down into smaller, related sections that are relevant to the
objective of the day. This effort to plan classes into 'chunks' was common
practice at schools on a block schedule because it was an effective method
of building relevance with students and helping teachers manage a longer
class period.

Although nervous, Anna was also excited about the prospect of sharing
valuable information with colleagues. The training sessions had led her to
reflect on her own lesson planning. And when incorporated into her class-
room, they immediately improved student engagement. Sharing this impact
on her own instruction was a major part of the presentation.

Anna's seven slides would promote the practice of "chunking" learning
activities. But the part she looked forward to most was discussing how teach-
ers can leverage relationships with students to build up this much needed
relevance.

Anna walked slowly to the front of the stage. After a month of planning,
she knew the material was beneficial. She was ready. From the top step, she
began.

"At this point, it's important for us to consider how extending the
amount of time in class will affect our lesson planning...."

The first few slides were easy. Anna was prepared. At her first oppor-
tunity to glance at the clock, she was surprised to see the end of her fifteen
minutes approaching. Emboldened by this realization that she was nearly
finished, she began to look around the room to gauge interest.

After one scan through the crowd, it was obvious that their sit-and-get
format was yielding mixed results. Many teachers were still attentive, but
the group needed a break. Anna filed that fact away in her memory banks

and moved to her conclusion, an anecdote about an apathetic student's reaction to an ELA lesson she built around sportswriting.

And just like that, the story ended and Anna was finished. She experienced a bit of euphoria at completing the presentation. "Why was I so nervous?" she thought. "That was a piece of cake!"

But as she handed the clicker over, she looked at the front row and made eye contact with Ron, a member of her own English department. Ron smiled briefly as their eyes met, and then looked down at a paper that was lying on the table in front of him. He scribbled something at the top, reached over to a tall stack of papers and grabbed another one.

Anna immediately realized Ron had spent the entirety of her presentation grading essays. She was furious. And embarrassed. As she walked back to her seat, Anna resolved to never make such a fool of herself again.

Instructional Leadership

Volumes have been written about content-specific methods for improving instruction, but there are certain principles common to every educator. For the purpose of studying professionalism, which is common to every educator, we will assume a measure of expertise in your content specialty and focus on the principles we have in common across all classrooms.

Supporting a strong culture of learning means focusing on *everyone's* learning, which makes professional development a priority. It's unfortunate, but "PD" has been, for a long time, one of the most cringe-worthy terms in all of education, inducing more eyerolls than motivation. This is a shame, because true PD is a critical part of the teaching and learning that occurs in a school. When professionals prioritize learning together, students always benefit.

Establishing professional learning as a priority is essential to building a culture of learning. The only question to answer is: Just who, exactly, is responsible for leading it?

Who Influences Teaching and Learning in a School?

The answer? Instructional leaders. But when you read those two words, it's important to detach them from the traditional school hierarchy that places responsibility on a single person at the top of the pyramid.

Of course, in a healthy learning environment, the administrator takes ownership of this role. But instructional leadership is an act that any adult in the school can provide. When we meet someone who leads in this way, prioritizing serving others over themselves, we gravitate toward these people because they look out for us. And we couldn't care less about their title. We follow them because they willingly donate their time and expand their work to include our tasks. When a dead-line looms, we run past the boss to ask these servant leaders what they think.

> When a deadline looms, we run past the boss to ask true servant leaders for help.

Providing helpful professional learning for your colleagues can be an intimidating task. But it is the missing link in building credibility for any instructional leader. I'm certain that taking on the responsibility to teach the teachers prevents a lot of great educators from considering the move to administration.

That's a shame, because so many of them have great ideas about instruction, and decades of great student performance in their class-rooms to back it up. And, friends, there is a great need. Scores of administrators around the country would give their right arm for the instructional credibility and influence these classroom veterans hold over the teaching and learning that takes place in their school.

After a rough ending to her presentation, Anna couldn't see past Ron's lack of professionalism. To do all that work, endure the stress of going in front of her peers, revealing personal struggles; and then have a colleague disrespect her like that just wasn't worth it. From her point of view, the return on that investment had to be zero.

Or so she thought.

Anna soon found herself in more and more conversations about instruction, with colleagues she didn't even know that well. It turns out quite a few people in the group were paying attention that day. Stepping out and offering to help in a PD session didn't move her up the school district ladder (at least not immediately), but it did elevate her standing among colleagues.

It wasn't the research, or the style of PowerPoint that did it, though. Anna put in the work, ignored the butterflies, and gave her best effort to serve. Some of her colleagues did learn the lesson on chunking, but the biggest takeaway was that she was just up there, willing to help her friends do their jobs better by sharing what she had learned.

Service. That's the main requirement for instructional leadership that improves a school. And students reap all the benefits.

A Culture of Collaboration

Traditional ideas about leadership, dictated by the location of a name on the organizational chart, are outdated. Authority might have to be delegated in this way, but instructional leadership certainly should not be.

Teachers most definitely play a role in leading the instruction in their schools. But they don't have to lead a large-group professional development session to do it. They can just walk across the hall and connect with a colleague. Then, work with them to improve instruction and help students learn.

At some point in the future, one of those attempts will work really well. Then, they will share it. A school culture that is devoted to teaching and learning will celebrate educators who share those discoveries

THE FIVE PRINCIPLES OF EDUCATOR PROFESSIONALISM

with the group. In a profession that places its key players on an island, we need leaders who do their climbing by serving and connecting. Let's count that type of collaboration as a major component of educator professionalism.

Think about the overall impact of one group of teachers getting off their islands and sharing the responsibility to improve instruction this year. They wouldn't have to follow some enigmatic process that requires a $100/hour expert. They simply need to have regular conversations about developing instruction, implementing formative assessments, selecting relevant content; and creating good transitions, hooks, and exit tickets. They compare assessment outcomes and regularly discuss ways to reteach missed content. They meet as a group to figure out what type of paragraph earns an A, or what type of thought process earns credit on an Algebra problem. And when they try something new, they figure out a way to observe each other's classes and hone those lessons to perfection.

Taking the initiative to start these conversations is how we serve our colleagues and improve our schools. When leaders refuse to limit themselves to the authority of their position, and make these valuable connections with colleagues, schools improve. Elevating everyone else's game in this way proves the old cliché all over again…Anyone can be a leader.

As Anna reflected on her first experience in leading professional development, and providing instructional leadership, she realized it made her a better teacher. But she also experienced two foundational truths about professional learning in a school:

1. For teachers, sharing with colleagues proves just how right Richard Elmore was when he famously claimed that *"Isolation is the enemy of improvement."* (Elmore, 2000, p. 20) It is evident that collaboration is the strongest driver of effective teaching and meaningful learning in a school. If isolation is the enemy of improvement, then collaboration is the lifeblood of it.

2. For administrators (and any other PD presenters), anytime you lead professional development for teachers, you'd better bring it. Teachers are the toughest crowd because they expect presenters to practice what they preach. Differentiate the professional learning in the same way we expect teachers to differentiate learning for their students. And for goodness sake, make it applicable to the classroom.

A Culture of Reflection

It should make sense that *professional* development would figure heavily into professional conduct at a school. After all, if educators are serious about learning, they should model that in their work.

But student achievement is the language everyone speaks. When the bell rings, and the classroom door slams shut, there will be twenty-five (or more!) sets of eyes trained on the teacher. The learning that takes place before the next bell makes all the difference in the world. That's the teaching and learning that ultimately determines the success of a school. The connection between a school and its community is up for grabs in there, too.

But there is one guarantee in that process. Students will not be forced into learning. For that classroom full of students to experience a successful year, they will need a teacher who plans meticulously and understands one of the most basic building blocks of a professional culture of learning—reflection.

Creating an environment that is simultaneously challenging, yet free from risk, is what makes teaching such a tough job. We chose this job because of our desire to serve as a mentor and advocate for students. But our ability to empathize, express concern, and encourage, while developing students' potential, is why this profession called us.

Reflection is the way we teach ourselves how to meet these daily expectations. If obstacles continue to stifle the process of challenging all students all the time, consider these steps as a starting point. Arriving at step five means you've earned the right to call your classroom a challenging learning environment for every single student.

Reflection is the way we teach ourselves how to meet these daily expectations.

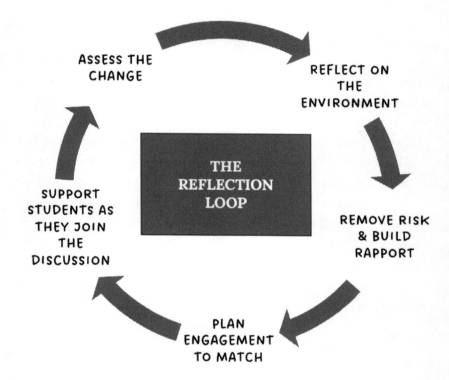

ASSESS THE CHANGE

REFLECT ON THE ENVIRONMENT

THE REFLECTION LOOP

SUPPORT STUDENTS AS THEY JOIN THE DISCUSSION

REMOVE RISK & BUILD RAPPORT

PLAN ENGAGEMENT TO MATCH

Congratulations, now you get to go back to step one and start over. People often say, "The grind never stops" when talking about teaching. When we consider reflection, it really shouldn't. Run through this loop several times a month and you will have experienced one successful year.

1. **Reflect on your classroom and assess the environment.** Use a student's point of view to reflect on your classroom and make an honest evaluation of the learning environment. Ask yourself some hard questions:
   a. How would students rate their comfort level in my classroom?
   b. Who doesn't participate?
   c. Could I sit through my lesson plan as a student?
   d. Is student behavior meeting my expectations? Are my expectations high enough?
   e. Did I tell them what behavior I expect on Day 1? Did I follow through with my consequences?
   f. Do I have a good relationship with the different subgroups of students in my classroom?
   g. Which groups shy away? This is the time to think long and hard about apathetic students who play everything off, saying, *"I Don't Care"* to mask deep misunderstanding or an even deeper personal problem.

2. **Remove risk.** Now, start the process of connecting with those students you missed. One of the most important things a teacher can do for their students is build rapport and remove the risk associated with allowing others to see them in a moment of misunderstanding.
   a. Learn student interests. Find out what makes them tick. Find a way to speak their language.
   b. Build on that rapport by incorporating healthy communication among students and with you into your lessons. Plan activities that make it easy to ask questions. This means creating opportunities for student interaction and facilitating dialogue.

c. Be persistent. Quite often, it will take several one-on-one conversations to melt away the front that apathetic students put up.

d. Never forget, sarcasm is dangerous in a classroom. Biting comments can destroy even the best learning environments for students who are hesitant to buy into what you are selling. Sarcastic comments might bring laughs and create comfort for the groups you connect with, but those outsiders will assume it is pointed at them. Sarcasm can then become an excuse to further separate themselves from the class.

3. **Plan engagement that matches interests.** Use the newfound rapport to add relevance to your lessons. This is a difficult step because it requires self-discipline and consistency.

a. Plan meaningful, engaging, bell-to-bell activities. A professional never deviates from bell-to-bell routines in their class.

b. Do this EVERY SINGLE DAY OF THE SCHOOL YEAR.

c. All interruptions to instruction are a problem to address immediately. Let one interruption or distraction slide, and you will soon have an unruly group.

4. **Support students who are learning to meet new challenges.** Removing risk and creating a well-managed environment opens the door for healthy classroom communication. Questioning technique is important here.

a. The goal should be a classroom where misunderstanding and confusion aren't stressful, and failure isn't final. Learning is based upon questioning, not the grade at the top of the paper.

b. If students know they can trust you—which means they know your WHY—and are comfortable admitting they need help, you've reached an important milestone. Pat yourself on the back.

c. Model your own learning. It's OK to make a visible mistake and work through it.

d. Reaching Step 4, where students in the back corner are participating as much as the ones on the front row, is a major accomplishment. People have literally gone decades without making it this far!

5. **Maintain the environment.** The only thing tougher than getting to Step 4 is staying there. Assessments play a critical role in this step.

a. Plan the right balance of formal and informal assessments in your classroom like a composer writing a piece of music. Employing the right assessment at the right time is a fine art. Incorporate too many formal assessments, and your classroom becomes a testing center. Shy away from them too often and you will go into tests blind, and bad grades will be a surprise.

b. Continue the self-reflection that got you here.

c. Go back to Step 1 and start this reflective process over again.

Achieving Equity Through Reflection

There's an awful lot of talk these days about achieving equity. And some of it can be distracting. Depending on who you ask, you might be told that this crucial mindset is a buzzword, an ideal, or a pejorative. Baruti Kafele (2021) provided a useful guide when he stated, "Equity isn't something you do. It's who you are." (p. 18) This only works if you mean it on Day 1, and every other day that follows.

51

If equity is part of our core, it means that the focus on learning covers every desk in the classroom, for every minute of class time. Following the steps to create a challenging learning environment that includes all students is how a teacher creates a classroom in which every single kid is valued and validated. Call it whatever you'd like, but that's why we are here: Every. Single. Kid. Every. Day.

When you get down to it, equity is about expectations. And for all the talk about them, your class roster is the least likely place to display an equitable set of expectations. What does success look like to each kid on your roster? Well, it's complicated. This complication is what makes teaching such an intimidating proposition.

There may be no more important reason for continuous reflection on the classroom environment than in the effort to achieve equity. Removing risk creates the opportunity for relationships that break down barriers to higher expectations.

So, what type of relationship do we want to build? We began the answer to that question back in Chapter Two, with Jimmy Casas's explanation of our core. Let's use his powerful description as a starting point, and progress toward achieving equity from there.

Achieving Equity Through Relationships

+ Start the relationship with our WHY. Invite students in to see our core, and build the relationship based solely on that fact. Personal information isn't nearly as important as purpose. *"I'm in this classroom with you because my purpose is to see each and every one of you grow. That might not be easy, but I'm here with you for the long haul."*

+ Continue on to the next step, understanding the varied student backgrounds, expectations, and ability levels that are present. *"Now that you know why I'm here, and you understand my expectations as a teacher, let's work through this activity that tells me about you.*

+ Build off those backgrounds, point out their abilities, and prepare them for the next step. *"I could see your ability as we solved all those equations. And that's good, because you'll need those strengths to tackle this next unit, solving multi-step equations. They are a tougher version of the same problem."*

Now, let's stop right here for a second. Because the next logical step is to move into a more rigorous objective. There will no doubt have to be some critical feedback involved as we uncover student mistakes and work to correct them.

But in the conversation on equity, which seeks to shrink achievement gaps in disadvantaged groups of students, those disadvantaged students are the least likely to trust educators to serve their best interests. Regardless of their reasons for struggling at school, those prior experiences will be translated directly onto you. I've included some hypothetical statements here to illustrate attempts a teacher might make to build these relationships up. But building trust takes time. You won't build this bridge in a day.

This fact is spelled out in some interesting research, which states that feedback and criticism of work are typically seen by disadvantaged students as reinforcement of negative stereotypes, unless the students feel as though they can trust their teacher.

So, before we can proceed to the critical step of feedback, and make the crucial step of minimizing achievement gaps, we must look deep within ourselves. If achieving equity is truly important to us, we must answer these two crucial questions with a resounding YES:

1. *"In my heart, do I truly believe my students are capable of more rigorous work?*
2. *"Do my students know in their heart that I believe in them?"*

It's all about expectations. We can't raise them unless we've built the proper relationship with students and secured their trust in us to guide them to that higher level. (Yeager, 2013)

Now, let's proceed.

+ Critique their mistakes with timely and appropriate feedback. *"This is the difficult aspect of solving multi-step equations. You missed this problem because dividing by a negative here changes the sign of the answer. You forgot to do that. This is what makes finding a solution difficult. Look at it this way…"*

If we are serious about reaching every student, removing risk is a requirement. The more varied the backgrounds in your classroom, the harder this will be to achieve. The differences are what bring out discomfort in kids. And when they aren't comfortable learning in a class, many other behaviors come out.

Once risk is removed, relationships can then fill the void. This makes purposeful, honest reflection a key component of equity. Identifying sources of discomfort for students can't happen without deep, honest reflection.

Defining the teacher's role in terms of the professional responsibilities of teaching and learning can go on and on when considering the learning environment. But of all the techniques and tricks that a teacher might have at their disposal, reflection might be the most effective method for improving practice. Without it, we will never achieve equity. It is a constant in classrooms that continually improve, which makes it another expectation for educator professionalism.

Using Data to Drive Instruction

There are few moments in the life of a teacher as exhilarating as the realization of a well-planned, well-delivered lesson that hits the mark with students across an entire classroom. When you notice students sitting on the edge of their seats, engaged in precisely the activity you selected to motivate them to learn, it's a joy that is difficult to explain to outsiders. I imagine the architect who drew up the Empire State Building feeling that same high as they opened its doors for the first time.

I remember this euphoria from my own American History classroom, in a lesson about Sergeant Alvin York's exploits in World War I. The interactive lecture I employed to discuss the importance of the Congressional Medal of Honor wasn't the highest priority according to our curriculum framework. But after much trial and error of learning to craft a good lecture, and building a relationship to understand my students, I was able to compose a lesson that played to their interests and aided student understanding of key curriculum objectives.

In other words, I learned to add relevance. What a difference maker.

Reflecting on what works, or what doesn't, in a lesson is how teachers turn students into their own little instructional coaches. There's no reason to wait on an administrator or coach to observe a classroom. Just read student reactions to the content and adjust accordingly. Before long, they'll be sitting on the edge of their seats, hanging on every word.

Creating an environment in which students are comfortable admitting they are confused is the tipping point in the reflective process of challenging every student. When kids are invested enough to honestly participate and share their struggles, they are in your corner.

In a professional's classroom, questions serve as cues to inform the teacher on the effectiveness of their instruction. If the kids aren't asking any questions, that's an important cue as well. That means it's probably time to up the level of rigor or go back to step one and begin the reflection loop all over again. Questioning, and any other data that informs on student misunderstanding, is how we improve instruction.

So, what drives good instruction? Once reflection becomes a regular practice, the professional leverages student relationships to anticipate student understanding (or misunderstanding). In this mode, assessments don't just produce a number at the top of the page, they inform teachers on how that data can be used to tailor the next lesson to meet student needs. Armed with this information, a real pro will consistently know the answer to the critical question of, "*What Drives My Instruction?*"

A better way to ask that question, though, might be to say, "*How often should I assess students over the course of one unit?*" If the only answer is a unit test, then students are missing out. Their grades will probably be lower than they should. And even worse, those low grades will be unexpected.

It's unfortunate, but the industrialized version of school that we work in today has separated the idea of measuring student understanding away from the act of instruction and turned a crucial portion of teaching and learning–assessment–into a dirty word. (When you read that word, there's a good chance you really thought of *standardized testing* though.)

This is a crying shame, because assessment should serve as a classroom speedometer, an invaluable part of a teacher's personal dashboard. True assessments match to each instructional activity, informing the teacher on student understanding, while they are in mid-delivery.

Unfortunately, assessment isn't the only word we've allowed legislators, bureaucrats, and testing companies to redefine for us. An even more egregious example is the word "Growth." It's not a number, and it's not the same for each kid, despite what our accountability models tell us. And it really can't be determined by a single test.

Growth is determined by parents, teachers, and students, working together to chart progress and maturity. And it is most definitely a moving target. Stephen Covey's definition of growth is more appropriate for the learning environment we all aspire to create. He related it to the concept of potential in *The Seven Habits of Highly Successful People* (1989).

"Growth is the process of releasing potential and developing talents, with the accompanying need for principles such as patience, nurturance, and encouragement." (Covey, p. 34, 1989)

"Patience, nurturance, and encouragement." Have you ever described a standardized test by any of those three actions?

The big, cold, heartless idea of standardized "Capital-A" Assessment is not what drives the instruction in a classroom. That feedback comes too infrequently. Standardized testing has its place, and the aspect of mobility that it offers students who can earn a high score to improve their odds of a better life is important. But for teachers, there is a much more appropriate and effective source of data at their disposal. "Small a" assessment, when used appropriately, is what drives instruction.

The sooner a teacher can notice a kid's confusion; the sooner they can attack that confusion from a different angle and bring the student along the learning continuum. Adjusting course based on instant feedback from formative assessments is how this is done. That is the way a real pro measures growth in a classroom.

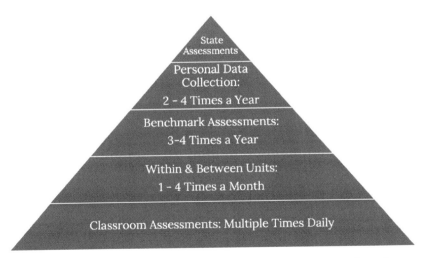

The larger the section on this assessment pyramid, the more often those assessments should be conducted. (Love, Stiles, & Mundry, 2008)

Solid formative assessments can change a good classroom into a great one. But the best instruction, delivered in the most engaging format possible, isn't a teacher's best lesson if the impact isn't measured.

Spending two weeks on a classroom adaptation of "The Greatest Show (in Science)" without checking for understanding multiple times along the way is likely to yield a low average score on the unit test and serve as a colossal waste of planning time.

Instructional activities that aren't paired with assessments will never be enough, by themselves, to yield learning. It really isn't *The Greatest Show* until you know, for a fact, that the students are getting what you are teaching. That means linking formative, or informal, assessments to instructional activities.

If you only rely on spreadsheets and score reports from the benchmark or end-of-course assessments, your students are missing out on some valuable learning. This data-filled, scientific approach to teaching couples well with the concept of the art of teaching. And there is definitely a fine art to a teacher adjusting instruction as they feel their way through a unit. Using expertise and judgment mid-lesson allows a teacher to deliver content to struggling students immediately.

Want your lessons to come alive? Employ more informal assessments. The point isn't that unit tests and the big, standardized assessments aren't valuable. Data from these summative assessments should certainly be reviewed regularly. Commonly missed objectives must be retaught to help students meet graduation requirements. But all assessments, big and small, fit together to drive instruction in a solid culture of learning.

Innovation, A Fancy Word for Trial-and-Error

A culture of learning that is free of risk for the student should also be free of risk for the professionals. Collegial support for teachers creates an environment in which trying new things in the classroom is encouraged. Innovation, or creating a new practice by improving on a prior standard, has become one of the trendiest buzz words ever. Education is no exception. Whether you are inventing something new or taking something established and transforming it into the cutting edge of a new industry, innovation must be boiled down to its simplest terms to be practiced.

Teachers practice innovation all the time. They just don't always use the fancy name for it. Innovation is a technical name for the trial-and-error process. A classroom doesn't have to look like Edison's engineering lab to be innovative. A teacher just starts with a problem, proposes an idea to solve it, then tries that idea out. Then, they choose some reasonable metric (assessment) to see if it worked. Finally, they make the necessary changes and try it again. That's it. A four-step process for innovation that serves as another key activity for professionals in a strong culture of learning.

The Trial-and-Error Innovation Loop
1. **Try out a new idea .**
2. **See if it worked.**
3. **Make changes.**
4. **Try again.**

Unfortunately, the natural reaction to the challenge posed by a classroom full of students is survival mode. Spending most of your days hovering just above fight-or-flight status stifles any attempt at innovation. (Also known as improvement.)

So, when a new teacher finds an activity that works, they hold on to it for dear life. It becomes a go-to. How they find these activities doesn't matter. They just know that they better find them quickly. All's fair in love and your first year of teaching.

We've already mentioned that isolation serves as a barrier to improvement. It also slows the innovation process to a halt by solidifying the processes of planning and teaching to the point of collecting and saving everything that worked and then standing pat. There's no time for reflection when you're in survival mode. Every action is reactive. The path of least resistance is preferred.

Have I described your first year in the classroom yet?

But getting through that initial year is an accomplishment that can easily lead to a feeling of self-sufficiency. This can seem like a good method for reducing the stress associated with teaching. But old lessons don't always help new groups of kids. Students might earn good grades in an environment that lives off old ideas that used to work. But kids in the other classrooms leave them behind in real-world application.

When teachers isolate themselves from their peers and resist changing old methods, it makes school improvement nearly impossible. And the students will behave wonderfully as you all travel down the achievement rankings together.

Where did that great activity you borrowed from the teacher down the hall get its start? Follow the trail back up the hallway, to the teacher who shared it with you, and then to the teacher across the county who shared it with them. How far would that trail lead? If you had the time to investigate the use of that "new" activity, you'd eventually end up in a classroom where a teacher had an idea, tried it for the first time, made some changes, and tried it again.

And when it worked, they decided to share it with a colleague. That's the power of trying, failing, trying again, and staying focused on finding a new solution to an old problem. Innovation.

For any of you grad school warriors out there, this is your bread-and-butter. The four step innovation loop also describes action research. Find a problem, try a solution, see if it worked. Then, write it up at night after the kids go to bed. For those keyboard warriors who like to decry the perceived lack of value in the Doctorate of Education, they are simply showing their ignorance of the work it takes to improve instruction for an entire classroom of kids, across an entire school.

The Ed.D. is a practitioner's degree, for people in the trenches of education. The servant leader who earns it isn't a researcher. And they aren't making claims to expertise in other fields. That task is reserved for people who criticize selfless service. But those that earn those three initials after their name have most certainly earned the title of *Doctor*.

Consistently making time to share with colleagues and reflect on what works is how we truly innovate within the field of education. Try it with your colleagues. It could change the trajectory of your school this year. That is the professional conduct that builds trust in the teaching and learning that takes place in a school community.

A Word on Lesson Planning

The one professional responsibility that is present at every step along this path to effective teaching and meaningful learning is lesson planning. Scripting classroom time and linking student activity to content objectives are the building blocks of a successful classroom. There may be no more important work done in support of instruction.

You may have noticed in our discussion on instruction, reflection, and assessment that most of those principles mirror the four big questions that are addressed by professional learning communities. Good lesson planning brings teachers together to focus on these foundational questions.

> What do we want students to learn?
> How will we know when they've learned it?
> How do we reteach if they didn't?
> How do we extend the lesson when they do?
>
> (Dufour and Marzano, p.23, 2011)

61

When teachers reflect on their work with colleagues, look at data and work together to address student needs, great lesson plans are the result. Managing classroom instruction that engages students in meaningful reading, writing, interaction, and appropriate assessment can't happen without this intentional process.

But lesson planning is a sore subject for many. Have you heard the old joke about them? It shines a light on the source of that frustration:

If an inbox 'dings' when a lesson plan is submitted, but the principal never opens the file, did it really ever make a sound?

Lesson planning isn't really the problem for true professionals. It's lesson planning that is required to fit some administrator's preferred format, submitted at a designated time, and then ignored. That is a problem. Hours of hard work, done solely for the purpose of documentation, that are then summarily disregarded, only to create an "Unread" notice in an administrator's inbox creates one of the strongest negative undercurrents in a school culture.

Lesson planning to check a box is a key feature of a weak culture of learning. And in cultures of isolation, check boxes exist everywhere because survival is the goal. Effective teaching and meaningful learning rarely happen when teachers stay in survival mode, though. When teaching plans are solidified into "what we used last year," survival is the best possible outcome.

A calendar of topics won't do it. A pacing guide, as helpful as that can be, won't do it either. It must be a daily plan for student success.

There may be no more applicable use of the phrase, *Simple, but not easy*. Follow these steps to improve your lesson planning:

+ Decide which learning objective should be taught.
+ Spell out student activities that lead students to think about and work through the objective.

+ This is the point where students are DOING something. Bloom's taxonomy of actions usually describes these student actions. You may have seen that list before.
+ This is also the point where experience is worth more than gold, because the amount of time it takes students to complete these activities makes all the difference in the world. Good lesson planning is a small-scale trial-and-error process in itself.
+ Assess student progress in each of these activities.
+ Reteach the deficiencies.
+ Still struggling? Log onto your favorite AI language model and ask it to generate one for you. You'll receive a basic plan instantly!

Along the way, you pick up tricks to correct for the variance in student abilities, which is where your colleagues come in. Work smarter, not harder, in lesson planning. Reflecting on good practices with a group of colleagues is the purpose of collaboration. After talking out the best method for attacking that next unit, take *that* plan to the principal. Put it in their spreadsheet, draw it on a treasure map, or get a tattoo of it. No self-respecting administrator (who wants to keep their job) will ever protest a lesson plan that is created by teachers who plan, analyze data, and innovate together.

So, should teachers be required to submit lesson plans regularly? Perhaps. But only if there's an ~~administrator~~ instructional leader there who's willing to read them, use them as a guide during observations, and then offer feedback to lead improvement.

Guiding Principles of Professionalism for Teaching and Learning

If we define professionalism as an educator's personal contribution to the culture of learning, it should go without saying that a devotion to the craft of instruction and assessment should be job number one on everyone's daily to-do lists. Professionals must dedicate themselves to student and professional learning in that effort.

However, the preceding topics on teaching and learning in this chapter are contingent on one major assumption: content knowledge. It isn't just important to be a content expert, it's everything. Having secured that foundation, we move into the other aspects of maintaining a culture that constantly promotes teaching and learning.

Instructional leaders know how to maintain a focus on reflection, collaboration, data-driven decision making, and innovation. This is how schools strengthen their culture of learning. But another reason to consume ourselves with these activities is that they also prevent us from making mistakes.

Legal and ethical professional conduct related to an employee's commitment to effective teaching and meaningful learning is mostly a matter of individual school district policy. Regardless of the guidelines, most every evaluation instrument requires an administrator observing an educator's practice at work. This means each individual educator should take the responsibility to understand their district and school-level expectations for maintaining competence in content, planning, collaboration, teaching practices, classroom management, and professional development.

Commitment to these principles is how a school culture fortifies itself against obstacles to good teaching and learning. Additionally, a commitment to professional learning is the catalyst to creating a strong culture of learning in a school. These actions speak loudly to the school community, showing parents our commitment to creating an environment in which kids are comfortable learning.

With that commitment secure, parents can trust us to stand in their place as caretakers of learning. Then, we can proceed to the next, and equally important, issue that builds trust within a school community.

Safety.

CHAPTER 5

Remain Vigilant

"**H**i, Miss Thompson! You ready for that lab today?"
"Absolutely! You're going to love dissecting a frog!"
"GROSS!"

Kristy Thompson, a veteran Biology teacher at Southside High, chuckled at her students' reaction—curiosity mixed with disgust. Her first block girls were regulars at this entrance. And like clockwork, they started every day with something nice to say about her class.

Some people might stress over an assignment to supervise student arrival. But for Miss Thompson, talking to kids and greeting them was just another great part of her job.

Eventually, she encountered Terri Floyd, a student who was dealing with an angry boyfriend, and asked for an update.

"Miss Thompson, these girls have texted me all weekend wanting to fight. And my boyfriend saw the messages. Last night, he got into a fight with one of the girls' brothers! One of those girls jumped in and kicked him! Can you believe that?"

Kristy stated the obvious, "This is terrible! Do your parents know about this?" Terri was no stranger to drama, but this situation was out of the norm.

Her voice quivered. "Yes. They called the police, but I'm scared he's gonna do something."

Kristy knew this angry boyfriend went to another school. Hopefully, that separation would minimize the drama for everyone else. She saw the principal and sent Terri his way. "You need to tell Dr. Quick about this immediately."

When the bell sounded, the hallway flooded with kids inching their way to class. That's when Kristy felt her phone vibrate. A parent had emailed last night to complain about her handling of a discipline issue. A quick check of her phone showed yet another reply. She immediately stepped aside and engrossed herself in another long, angry parent email.

~

Melvin Jones's day began in a much different way, contemplating how to remove a shattered bathroom mirror without hurting himself. "Mr. Melvin," as he was affectionately known, enjoyed the early morning silence of a school.

As he carefully lifted the mirror off its bracket, hundreds of tiny shards of glass fell into the trash bin. A military retiree turned custodian; Melvin had seen a lot in two decades at his alma mater. But the conversation he'd just interrupted was troubling.

After walking in with the new mirror, two boys entered behind him discussing a student named Terri and a boy from another school. They'd described him as a jealous boyfriend and talked about a fight video being shared on social media. Evidently, the boyfriend hadn't fared too well in the altercation. Melvin detected worry in their tone, which was out of character for typical teenage boy talk.

With a new mirror in place, Melvin moved to his usual morning spot, the cafeteria stage. From this vantage point, the old custodian and the young coach watched kids eat breakfast and became intrigued by an interaction in the hallway. They could see Miss Thompson and a female student involved in an animated conversation.

"There's something in the air...You can feel it. It's louder than usual." Melvin commented.

Coach Hardy agreed, "Yes sir, there is definitely a buzz in the air. I saw it yesterday at practice. The boys were talking about a fight that happened over the weekend. That's the girlfriend over there now with Miss Thompson. There's a kid from another school involved, and he is bad news. Stays in trouble with the law. It sounded like she's playing the two boys off each other, which makes it worse."

Melvin continued to watch Miss Thompson and Terri. Coach Hardy's observation didn't ease his worries. As he looked across the cafeteria into the hallway, he could see Terri walking away from Miss Thompson. They were both staring at their phones with puzzled looks on their faces.

At that moment, the cheer squad interrupted the scene, running for the exit. Their coach followed close behind and propped open the exit door with a wet floor sign. For the next five minutes, cheerleaders ran back and forth from the coach's van to the cafeteria stage, stacking boxes of uniforms. When the bell rang, the girls dropped everything and headed up the hallway together.

The young coach started toward the gym. "Mr. Melvin, I'll see you later."

"Yes, sir, Coach. See you at lunch." Melvin said, still focusing on the hallway. He couldn't believe what he was seeing. Miss Thompson had started up the hallway to her classroom. As she walked, she showed her phone to the cheer coach and held her palms up in the air, obviously frustrated. Both were headed to class, oblivious to the propped entrance door behind them. When Melvin looked back at it, the word "CAUTION" glared at him like a neon light. He shook his head and walked toward the door. It was the third time this month he'd had to do this.

As Melvin approached the door, a car zoomed up to the curb outside. A young man hopped out and jogged up the long sidewalk toward the door. He was carrying a heavy backpack by his side. Through that door, Melvin could clearly see a large bruise on the boy's right eye that made the scowl on *his face look even worse. The events of the week tumbled into place for the Southside custodian.*

Melvin sprinted the final three steps to the doorway and jerked the caution sign away, slamming the door shut. The young man, about to pull something out of his backpack, froze as the door closed in his face. For a brief second, they faced each other through the glass door. Melvin could see something metallic in the boy's hand, and then backpedaled up the hallway. He immediately grabbed his radio, "OFFICER MCGEHEE, COME TO THE SOUTH ENTRANCE IMMEDIATELY! DOCTOR QUICK, DO YOU COPY?"

The young man turned and ran.

~

Three hours later, the lockdown ended. For the students that hadn't already checked out of school, lunch began. As everyone filed into the cafeteria, the buzz continued. But the topic had shifted to the police response to an intruder.

Coach Hardy moved back onto the stage. Instead of his usual partner, Officer McGehee was on duty with him today. Coach had witnessed Melvin's act of bravery from the other end of the long hallway, so their conversation rehashed the eventful morning at Southside. "Boy, Melvin saved us today, didn't he?"

Officer McGehee, having spent the past two hours watching footage of the incident, gave a full play-by-play, "We almost had a nightmare scenario on our campus this morning. We had a teacher prop open an exit door and leave it unattended; a teacher supervising the open doorway missed it because she was lost in her cellphone; and an armed intruder arrived on campus with every intention of harming students. Thank God we had old Melvin in that hallway. He was a cool customer."

He paused to stop two kids from pushing each other in the line, then continued. "You know, a lot of people talk about preventing a crisis, but that's all they do. Talk. Melvin put everything together before the police could. Dispatch didn't understand the calls warning us about this kid last night. If Melvin hadn't kept his guard up and connected all the dots, someone would've gotten hurt today."

> If you want to know what's going on in a school, it would be smart to talk to the custodian. They notice everything.

Coach Hardy nodded along and added his own take. "I've worked with Melvin for ten years now, and I can tell you one thing: If you want to know what's going on in a school, it would be smart to talk to the custodian. They notice everything."

Nightmare Scenarios

Check your news feed. The odds are good that an article about school safety will pop up. Or, God forbid, a report from a new incident of school violence. Regardless of the content, the odds are also pretty good that you—being an educator—will click it and read. We can't help it; we are drawn to the topic.

School safety, a subject that used to cover wet floors, fights, and overly-sharpened pencils, has transitioned into dark territory. And no matter how hard we try, it's unavoidable.

As we sit in the dark, against a wall, awaiting an all-clear to end another active shooter drill, our thoughts usually gravitate toward the nightmare scenarios. *Pearl...Columbine...Sandy Hook...Parkland...are we next?* These thoughts rotate on a dark, infinite loop through our minds when we are faced with crisis response training. But the reality is worse than a nightmare.

Shouldering the responsibility of serving *in loco parentis* means that, above all else, we guarantee the safety of every student for the entire time they are in our care. And the fact of the matter is that our society isn't as safe as it used to be. Our willingness to work in a school means that physical safety is the foundational component of a school's culture. Supervising students and making every effort to prevent an unsafe situation is the first, and the most important, step educators take in building trust with our community. In assuming this role, we effectively tell parents, "*I agree to keep your kid safe.*"

Cross one of these boundaries and your career, or possibly even a child's life, could be in jeopardy. And your ability to effectively teach won't matter one bit.

But educators in the real world of a school—exposed daily as we work in the wide-open spaces of hallways, libraries, and cafeterias full of kids—face some serious obstacles to achieving a safe environment. We may not be able to arm ourselves as protectors (yet), and we don't have the impact that policymakers and politicians hold over this issue, but there is plenty for us to do. Our biggest challenges in securing schools are often the unseen forces of complacency, indifference, and—you guessed it—breakdowns in professional conduct.

Nonnegotiables

Educators are assigned many duties in a school that may be up for interpretation, but providing a safe and secure campus isn't one of them. Proper supervision, provided throughout the school day, is a *nonnegotiable* expectation for educators. If you're unfamiliar with the term, it's time to learn it. Nonnegotiable tasks are responsibilities that no one, from the custodian all the way up to the superintendent, can fail to uphold.

Standing *in loco parentis* means that we pledge to work together to ensure student safety, just like a good parent would. So a quick trip to the restroom, or a sprint down the hallway to make ten extra copies, is out of the question if it leaves students unsupervised. It means that any form of private or unmonitored communication with students is a non-starter.

Propping open an exterior door, or spending time on our cell phone during a supervision assignment aren't just actions to be frowned upon, they absolutely cannot happen. Nonnegotiable school safety protocols that keep students safe aren't suggestions to make us feel better, they are etched-in-stone guidelines that everyone must follow. Twenty-four-hours-a-day, seven days-a-week. Do them, or face dire consequences.

> **Nonnegotiable school safety protocols that keep students safe aren't suggestions to make us feel better, they are etched-in-stone guidelines that everyone must follow.**

Supervising students as they occupy an area before school, or travel to their next class—general supervision—is a critical time in the day for school safety. Granted, it might not be the most enjoyable activity on our to-do lists and isn't as constructive as classroom supervision, but observing students while they await the opening bell, eat lunch, or as they are dismissed, ensures student safety and is a foundational mission of every adult in the building.

Like many professional responsibilities, supervision is a simple activity. Stand in your assigned location. Watch children. Engage with them. Pay attention so you can give a good eyewitness account if something happens. And don't get distracted. (Put that cell phone away!) But for the educator trying to juggle several tasks at one time, it can be quite difficult to achieve. Multitasking is a dangerous activity when it comes to any aspect of educators' work, but even more so with supervision.

School safety and our previous topic, teaching and learning, are both urgent tasks that we consider extremely important to our work as educators. But urgency and importance can sometimes compete against each other. The work piles up and we often attempt to multi-task.

Professional conduct that promotes school safety begins with an understanding of the difference between urgency and importance, and how to decide which tasks take priority.

Dangerous Trade-Offs

In our safety scenario, Miss Thompson and the Southside Cheer coach failed this test. By prioritizing an angry parent email, and completing a task related to coaching responsibilities, both educators committed major errors in judgment and sacrificed the urgent needs of supervision and safety.

In Miss Thompson's case, she ruined a great morning of welcoming students to school by forgetting to supervise her area at a critical time. The biology teacher became distracted by an angry parent email and abandoned her post too early. And the cheer coach committed one of the most unforgivable sins on a school campus, leaving an unmonitored exit door propped open.

If not for a wise custodian watching the situation unfold, destructive and tragic violence may have occurred. Melvin's ability to remain vigilant, and prioritize tasks appropriately, saved the day.

Losing focus on *urgent* needs by jumping into an *important* task at the wrong time is a dangerous trade-off that can compromise school safety. Educators must make every effort to prevent this type of oversight from occurring, because most of these trade-offs directly weaken campus safety and security.

The dichotomy between urgency and importance is a timeless principle of leadership. Dwight Eisenhower, no stranger to tough decision making, perfectly summarized the leader's dilemma in a 1954 speech to the World Council of Churches:

> *"I have two kinds of problems: the urgent and the important.*
> *The urgent are not important, and the important are never urgent."*
> (Eisenhower, 1954)

Ike's quote is perfect because few leaders could speak with such authority on decision making. He was the only person whose resume was so impressive—three decades as an officer in the U.S. Army, Supreme Commander of Allied Forces in World War II, Military governor of Germany, and President of Columbia University—that many considered him overqualified for the White House. But while he stared at a map of Normandy, or deliberated with world leaders in the Oval Office, President Eisenhower struggled with the same leadership dilemma that Miss Thompson faced when an angry parent email landed in her inbox.

She made the wrong choice, and it almost cost her beloved students dearly. Were the contents of that email important? Absolutely. Was choosing to multitask while supervising student arrival a good idea? Absolutely not.

And the Southside cheer coach committed an even more egregious error. She prioritized convenience in stacking uniform boxes over keeping her school safe. Imagine trying to explain that decision to a parent whose child was injured by an intruder. When you consider the decision of urgency vs importance in that light, it's easy to see how administrators can sometimes lose their cool when they see a forgotten chair holding the door open for a parent meeting that ended three hours earlier.

Convenience should never be a priority over school safety. Ever.

A Threat of a Different Nature

But armed intruders aren't the only threats kids face. We must also remain vigilant to threats from within as well. This is an equally important feature of the trust a school community places in educators who would serve in their place.

When you scroll through your news feed, looking for school safety posts, you are equally likely to encounter a story exposing the actions of a person in a position of trust who ended their career by harming students through an inappropriate relationship. It is impossible to overstate the damage these situations can cause to a school community. Inappropriate educator-student relationships don't erode trust, they end it.

These unforced errors are so maddening that a former superintendent of mine, disgusted by the thought of dealing with another one of these awful incidents, once pleaded with over 1,500 employees during a convocation assembly, "Please, don't have sex with your students!"

You would think that would be a given. But as we've already mentioned, we can't assume anything these days. The shock value of the comment illustrated his point clearly.

Unmonitored, one-on-one communication between educators and students is usually how these types of traumatic situations begin, which is why this type of communication should be universally prohibited. And traumatic is the appropriate word; for the student, for the parents, for the family of the offending educator, and everyone else associated with that school.

Students are notoriously shrewd in face-to-face communication, sniffing out fake sincerity from a mile away. But get them online, interacting through text, and their radar can malfunction. Add in a teacher who doesn't respect their position of trust over students, and a cell phone conversation can become another tragic instance of a kid being in the wrong place at the wrong time. The emotional connection these encounters create makes disaster an eventual certainty.

I'm convinced that most of these encounters don't begin with a teacher crafting a detailed plan to groom a minor into an inappropriate sexual relationship. I'd like to think that the majority of these instances consist of a thousand small mistakes in the wrong direction. But for someone on the outside looking in, it sure appears that was the intention all along.

Personal, private communication that is in any way off-topic from an educator's professional responsibility is dangerous because it creates an environment that could lead to an inappropriate relationship. This type of communication by itself is just as dangerous as the physical act and violates everything related to our purpose of protecting kids.

So how do we prevent these situations?

Well, my superintendent's shocking comment isn't so far off base. School leaders (remember, that's all of us) need to talk openly and regularly about the dangers behind inappropriate communication and inappropriate relationships with students. Our agenda should be plainly transparent for all to see when it comes to student safety:

- Everyone on staff needs to be reminded, often, that no one is immune from violations in inappropriate communication or relationships. If we don't take this threat seriously, we are betraying the trust students and parents place in us.
- Open lines of communication between students, educators, and parents are critical in preventing violations and protecting students.
- Anonymous reporting should be offered freely.
- Consequences of these actions must be open knowledge for all employees and must be reviewed regularly.
- Principles of student safety must be on the agenda throughout the year, not just in the pre-service meetings before school starts.

The Threat of Intimidation

Students can also feel unsafe at school because of their classmates. Bullying, intimidation, and physical violence are all serious school safety issues.

The National Center of Educational Statistics (NCES, 2021) claims that 20% of students experienced some form of bullying or harassment in the 2017-2018 school year. I'm not here to dispute their procedures or metrics, but there is no way that number is an accurate picture of bullying in schools. Educators with any experience know that the unreported acts of bullying are prevalent and cause just as much damage. How much stress, anxiety, and learning loss can be attributed to the intimidation and harassment that goes unreported because a student fears retaliation?

Kids being mean to each other is another age-old problem that we have been tasked with solving. And there may be no other problem that can occur in a school for which culture is a more appropriate solution. Educators must support a culture of honesty that encourages open and truthful communication between students, parents, and educators—about any instance of bullying. We must remove the stigma of reporting these incidents as well, and be honest about the consequences.

The tricky part about addressing the scourge of bullying, and school violence, is the role that online communication plays. Social media platforms, which usually bring out the worst in everyone, tend to serve as an accelerant, bringing more attention to the impacted student and making the environment even more uncomfortable than it already is. School leaders (again, all of us) must take some specific steps to minimize the impact bullying and violence can have on the school environment:

+ Speak openly, and often, with students about specific consequences that aggressive behavior can have on the receiving student. Build relationships and lean on them to understand events on the ground. Engage with mental health professionals for guidance in this area, as it can quickly travel into dark territory.

+ Speak openly, and often, about the harms and potential consequences for aggressive and intimidating behavior. Cite chapter and verse from the student code of conduct as to how student aggression will be handled by the administration.

+ Communicate priorities and individual situations to parents as often as possible. Over-communication might not be possible in this area.

+ Again, make reporting as easy, and anonymous, as possible.

A Daily Approach to School Safety

Building relationships with students is the single best way to create a daily approach to school safety. These relationships don't just promote student learning; they are equally vital to keeping a school safe. Any assistant principal or counselor worth their salt will tell you that understanding body language and disposition is a huge component of getting to know students. You meet a kid, talk to them when they get off the bus, and pretty soon you understand their "baseline behavior." After a few days, you can read them without even asking a question.

And on the days when that typical behavior is off, it's time for a conversation. Whether you're investigating an incident, or addressing rumors of a potential threat, knowing the student on a personal level is how we keep schools safe.

Professional conduct that promotes school safety starts and ends with strong student relationships. Building them is one of the most proactive school safety measures an educator can take. Even if you don't know a student involved in rumors of a threat, you may still have a relationship with students who have knowledge. That knowledge can save the day.

- Notice student attitudes and dispositions.
- Get to know them personally.
- An attitude of constant awareness toward school safety is consumed with preventing violence. Listen to what students are saying.
- Promote positive student-teacher relationships, centered on learning and keeping the building safe.
- Teach appropriate interaction between students.

Mandatory Reporting

The role of mandatory reporter is another topic we don't discuss nearly enough in our professional learning. It serves as the structure for nearly all the business conducted on a school campus.

The level of reporting required of us starts off harmlessly enough. We don't usually discuss grades in the conversation on mandatory reporting, but that's the first step down this road to creating a safe environment that parents can trust.

Reporting home to parents about academic progress is the first aspect of mandatory reporting. Web-based grading systems that offer parents the option to check grades online don't absolve us of this responsibility. It just accelerates the timing of how schools and parents hold each other accountable. Entering grades in the gradebook is now a reporting mechanism for academic progress. Anyone who's had a child experience a precipitous drop in their average when a teacher becomes lax and then enters eight grades on the final day of a term understands this. Enter grades into the gradebook weekly (at a minimum) so students have an opportunity to improve their grade—and more importantly their learning—before a term ends.

But allowing access to grades doesn't scratch the surface. We want children to focus on learning, not just a number at the top of the paper. That means the environment, and student behavior within it, should be understood by parents too. A low grade can't communicate why it's low. So phone calls and parent conferences aren't just a good thing to do, they are an expected part of the educational process.

But these two actions can often be stressful for educators. We've all heard, and sometimes experienced, horror stories of parent conferences that went off the rails, or calls home that had to end abruptly. But most of the nervousness is just an exposure of the fact that we don't take these actions often enough to be comfortable with them. If a student steps out of line, or struggles continually, parents need to know. It's our responsibility to notify them. A phone call home is a must. If craziness occurs while you're in that conversation, it's time to back out and bring in an administrator. That's why they make the big bucks.

Email isn't necessarily a bad mode of communication for keeping parents informed, but it doesn't build the relationship nearly as well.

And that should always be our focus if we want to do what's best for children. Calling home, or requiring a parent conference to discuss poor behavior, performance, or attendance is how we partner with parents. These actions don't have to be contentious, even if a parent is defensive about the news. It's just a call home to ask for help.

Making time to call parents is a bedrock responsibility of the professional educator. If you are too busy to make phone calls home, then you are too busy. And it's totally fine to call them with good news every once in a while, too. Add time in your schedule for a positive phone call. I promise, you'll be glad you did.

> If you are too busy to make phone calls home, then you are too busy.

There is one more aspect to mandatory reporting that speaks to the vigilance that is required of educators to keep students safe. Sometimes, we learn information that a student has experienced abuse or other critical personal information about a student. If we become aware of this information, parent notification is required. And if the home environment is a possible source of the violence or abuse, we have a legal responsibility to protect that child by reporting it to the proper authorities.

These reports are not easy to make, but it's important to remember that the initial report merely shows the need for an investigation and doesn't assign any blame or consequences. In most cases, this just requires passing the information that was received along to a guidance counselor or administrator. But failing to make the report has the potential to keep abuse concealed and harm students. Additionally, it could bring liability on to the educator who hides the information. A professional would never take a chance of letting abuse continue, regardless of who might be angered at home.

Guiding Principles of Professionalism for School Safety

Safety and security are two constants in an educator's personal contribution to the culture of learning. The effort to maintain professionalism dictates a dedication to the safety of our students and our colleagues like our own lives depend on it. Heed all warnings carefully. There are volumes of state and federal legal code devoted to maintaining safety on a school campus. Educators must be fluent in these explicit guidelines and follow them daily.

Much of the responsibility for maintaining a safe campus is on us. If you aren't familiar with the guidelines for safety at your school, put this book down right now and go find your employee code of conduct or district safety policy immediately. Breakdowns of professional conduct in these areas can lead to tragic consequences, and constitute serious violations of the law.

Here are a few of the most serious principles of student safety for professional conduct. If you are balancing urgency and importance, this category would cover both. Everything stops if we encounter one of these situations:

- Engaging in child abuse or endangerment.
- Ignoring reports or threats of violence.
- Sexual relationships in any form–physical or online–with a student, regardless of their age.
- Sexual relationships, innuendo, or inappropriate joking with colleagues.
- Communicating inappropriately with a student, through any mode.
- Threats of any type that are directed at a student.
- Drug use in any form, with or without students present. Even if your state has passed laws that allow use of marijuana, or other

drugs, there is no justification for possession or use in a manner that would affect your work with children.

People who would commit these acts belong in jail. But there are other unethical behaviors that can be just as damaging to students and the school community. They may not immediately result in legal action but could certainly be deserving of reprimand, or termination of employment:

- Sexual remarks, innuendo, or jokes.
- Invitation to connection through social media or private text messaging.
- Ignoring reports of abuse, intimidation, or harassment.
- Failing to take action as a mandatory reporter when information relates to threats or abuse.
- Failure to provide appropriate supervision of students.

We each have different roles to play in the effort to keep schools safe, but remaining vigilant to the dangers present in our world today is our best method of keeping a school safe. This vigilance consumes us as we work to provide a safe school and create appropriate relationships with students and their families. Here are a few of the more constructive actions that should be mentioned when school safety becomes a topic of conversation:

- Open communication between students, teachers, and parents is an absolute necessity. Good schools make sure these three groups are always on the same page.
- Confidentiality regarding student information, or their activities, should be considered a pillar of school safety as well. Breaking confidentiality immediately ruins a family's trust in us.
- Professional learning is devoted to developing expectations for proper communication with parents and for maintaining a safe school environment.

+ Honesty between educators about the dangers of complacency
  is encouraged. This isn't just a professional learning expectation,
  but a daily interaction between educators. It's on every faculty
  meeting agenda and belongs on the posters we print and put up
  on our walls.

The best guidelines, by themselves, won't create or maintain a safe
school environment in which students can learn. That comes from professionals who take their work to prevent safety hazards seriously.

Complacency, which can damage a safe environment as badly as
the scariest intruder, must be defeated at all costs. One way to defeat
complacency, which can threaten safety and quite a few other priorities,
is through an action I've purposely been redundant in mentioning in
this chapter. Once the school environment is secured, it's time to focus
on an underrated aspect of developing trust: Understanding the power
of communication.

CHAPTER 6

Communication

Let's consider the work of serving *in loco parentis* in the simplest possible terms. If serving students and families represents *WHY* we are educators, then providing teaching, learning, and a safe environment would constitute *WHAT* we do at school. Extending this view of our work, communication would serve as *HOW* we conduct the business of educating children and serving families.

And that work entails lots of talking.

A village can't raise a child if the villagers don't trust each other. And it's impossible to trust someone you don't know. So, any effort to improve professional conduct must include a hard look at the only action through which everyone in a school community can understand each other: communication.

Now, you could fill the Grand Canyon with all the ink spilled explaining how to create a safe, effective learning environment. But in all those stories and studies, communication usually plays a supporting role, if it's mentioned at all. If we are ever going to understand our students, parents, and colleagues; and conduct ourselves as the professionals they all expect us to be we must excel at communication.

But just like every other aspect of working in a school, when you peel back the layers of this onion, it's complicated. When you consider a teacher's total count of interactions in a typical day you see why. There is so much of it. Facing the end of a school day and longing for a few minutes of peace and quiet is so important for this reason.

Let's break all those interactions down into three main categories: official communication, unofficial communication, and listening. Rank them however you wish, but understand that communities judge the effectiveness of their schools by how well their educators can do all three.

Communication that Encourages

Official communication, the proofed and edited messaging we promote every day, is everyone's first thought on this topic. Classroom lectures, emails, calendars, forms, documentation, and more, all delivered with the full authority of our positions behind them. We tend to think this is the most important form of communication, and rightly so. It's how we meet legal requirements to conduct teaching, learning, and safety procedures in our schools. Getting official communication right is an important reflection on our dedication to doing the work properly.

Most of the communication guidelines placed on educators dictate our actions in this mode. So, the nonnegotiables of official communication are many. Compliance with confidentiality laws that protect student information is a basic requirement. Notifying parents regularly about the progress and well-being of their children is another one. Purchasing procedures, a foreign concept for many who enter our field, carry a mountain of regulations that must be followed. Communications about assignments, assessments, and expectations carry the weight of a legal contract between teachers and their students.

Electronic communication is another important mode of official communication. Every message you type, whether an email or work-related text, should always be considered fair game for a lawyer to read back to you some day in the future. So make sure the content is appropriate. And never forget, the delete key is the most important one on the keyboard. Use it often.

Errors in official communication can be costly. Mess this form up by announcing incorrect information, firing off a harsh reaction by email, or violating the accommodations in a student's Individual Education Plan, and you can quickly run afoul of school policy, or even the law.

But the conversation about official communication doesn't just have to be a list of don'ts. Our actions speak loudly and constitute official messaging as well. Understanding this fact can add a new dimension to our work. True professionals make sure interactions between colleagues take place with a kindred spirit instead of a rival.

> True professionals make sure interactions between colleagues take place with a kindred spirit instead of a rival.

I learned how powerful official communication can become as a source of encouragement years ago when Janice, a veteran geometry teacher from down the hall, walked into my classroom just after the dismissal bell one day. She immediately began to call out names I remembered from the previous year, which was my first as a teacher.

"Do you remember teaching Ronnie, Bill, and Gerald in your Algebra class last year?"

"I sure do." I responded, immediately on guard. Those names brought back some bad memories. *"It sounds like you've inherited my third period from last year. I hope you have better luck with them than I did."*

Janice chuckled. *"Well, it's just the first week. They've been fine so far. I wanted to tell you, though, we spent most of today's class reviewing Algebra topics to see what the students retained from last year."*

Now I was officially worried. Those guys would spend weeks talking about everything *but* algebra in my class. I immediately recoiled at the idea of that group spouting off in another classroom about the mistakes I made last year, or attributing their weak knowledge of math to me. What an embarrassment.

"I wanted you to know they answered almost every question."

My jaw hit the floor.

In a full laugh by now, she finished her story. *"When I asked them how they remembered so much about solving equations and graphing lines, they yelled out in unison, 'Coach Lollar taught us this last year!'"*

I was in disbelief. Then, Janice took the conversation a step further. If I live to be ninety, I'll never forget it.

"In fact, they did such a good job today, I wrote the whole back-and-forth down and gave it to our principal to keep in your file. I wanted him, and you, to realize how much of an impact you made on those guys last year."

And just like that, she turned to leave.

I don't think Janice understood the impact she had on me that day. My shock eventually subsided, and I found the presence of mind to thank her profusely for her outreach. By noticing my efforts to teach a few hard cases, Janice made my year.

Showing a colleague the impact of their work is so much more effective than just saying, "Thank you." I never won any awards for my time in the classroom, but I can't imagine winning one that would give me the same sense of accomplishment I received that day.

Janice's unprompted act of kindness communicated that she valued my work as a teacher. And she used an official form of communication to do it. How good could this school year be if we looked for "official" ways to impact our colleagues and highlight their hard work the way Janice did? How good could a school culture become if the teachers supported students, and each other, in word and in deed?

We spend so much of our time in isolation, it can be easy to forget the positives. Your colleagues are doing great things every day. But it takes an extra effort to look up and take the time to notice them. And then, let them hear about it. How close could a school community grow if recognizing hard work and supporting students and colleagues was the norm for professional conduct within a school community?

Communication that Lasts

While official communication is crucial to the business of a school, unofficial communication might be even more significant. These are all the unplanned, spontaneous reactions that take place as you answer a random question before class, gossip in the workroom, react in the hallway, or text with your closest colleagues. Unofficial communication, often delivered through our attitude, is so important because it's how we tell people the truth.

> Unofficial communication, often delivered through our attitude, is so important because it's how we tell people the truth.

It's a bit intimidating to think that every idle word we utter, as we interact with hundreds of students every day over the course of our career, could become part of their life-long memory of us, or serve as motivation for their life's work. The sheer volume of interactions involved in a single day is staggering. Policing our speech in the flow of these conversations is unrealistic, but maintaining a focus on our purpose and attitude is.

Self-discipline with respect to our thoughts and attitudes helps us maintain perspective. And try as we might to conceal it, attitude always shows. So, with the proper mindset in place, quick reactions made in anger at a frustrating student become a little easier to prevent. Social media posts don't call our fairness into question.

Unofficial communication is huge for another reason: it can be dangerous. It has derailed many good teachers who reacted in a moment of weakness. When we maintain a proper focus on our attitude, the effect of our unofficial communication on students is profound, and makes an impact that can last far past our own careers. My high school baseball coach illustrated this effect by maintaining positive speech through a downright ugly situation.

~

It started, like it does with most good teachers, with "The Look." Coach Wood's was effective. He'd hold his hands out, purse his lips, and tilt his head in a way that would ask, *What are you thinking?*

He had a hilariously dry sense of humor, so the look would often be followed by a laugh. We imitated the look. But he didn't care. It got his point across. Coaches and teachers have more important things to worry about.

My senior season, only Coach Wood's second as a head coach, showed us the importance of his attitude, and rubbed off on us in the process. Unfortunately, he had to employ *The Look* quite often that year.

After an early season slump threatened to end our playoff hopes, the seniors on our team felt it was time for an intervention. As the losses piled up, we decided a team camping trip would be the exercise that could strengthen the bonds between players and translate into wins.

The adults didn't agree. Calls were made. Meetings held. Administrators consulted. And Coach Wood squashed the idea at the end of our next practice, promising severe punishment if we conducted a team activity without his permission. We didn't want to admit it, but he was right.

And the seniors reacted predictably. We thought we weren't being heard. In addition to dealing with poor play, Coach Wood now faced sour attitudes. This bout of immaturity wasn't his fault, but it created an atmosphere that folks today might describe as toxic.

The next game was critical. A victory could revive our fading playoff hopes. But the poor defense and weak hitting that started the problem continued. What we hoped would be a season-saving victory ended up as an embarrassing seven-run loss.

Coach Wood said his piece to us after the game. *"You guys are playing like you're more worried about camping than playing ball. Your mind is somewhere else. Talk it out as a team. When you can agree to do things the right way, we can go home. I'll let y'all decide."*

As he waited on us from the dugout, our players-only meeting sounded more like an argument. Leadership meant volume to us at that age. When the talk finally ended, we loaded our equipment—and our attitudes—on the bus and headed home. But first, we stopped to eat.

Naturally, the staff at the restaurant that night couldn't handle the crowd. A few of us were able to get our orders filled quickly, but the underclassmen got stuck at the counter as more customers rushed in. The delay was long. Adding hunger into the mix only made things worse. I'll never forget Coach Wood walking back into the dining area to address his team in Carthage, Mississippi, late on a Tuesday night.

Half the team was furious because they were hungry. The other half was mad at an extended delay on a school night. Everyone was dejected by the loss and tired. The recent turmoil still an elephant in the room. His response to this dejected group? *The Look.* Then, an observation, with his trademark sense of humor. *"Guys, what are we doing here? Are we camping out at McDonald's tonight?"*

Corny, for sure, but his timing was perfect. We erupted in laughter.

I'd love to report that we rallied and made the playoffs, but we didn't. Coach Wood's biggest victory in a season that ended with 13 wins and 14 losses was pulling his team back together.

Looking back, I realize now that we didn't imitate *The Look* so much after that night. Respect for our new coach was growing. And it is obvious now that the most powerful weapon at his disposal during those tough times was his attitude. He was always positive, which meant that his teams were always positive. His faith was apparent in the way he lived. I was around him nearly every day for two years and never once heard him utter a profane word.

You wanted Coach Wood's approval as a player, but you also wanted his approval as a person. His example pushed us to be better. One way to measure Coach Wood's impact would be the same way we measure all great coaches: through his players. Four guys that suffered through that losing season moved on to coach high school baseball. Coaches often talk about the low percentage of players that get to play at the next level after high school. But the percentage of players that go on to coach is even lower. You know those statistics well.

And three of those four future coaches were some of the same disgruntled seniors who saw the truth in our situation through Coach Wood's sense of humor. We admired his work so much that we followed in his footsteps.

The impact of one educator on the world is immeasurable. And that impact is delivered through their attitude. If you don't believe it, watch a graduate come back to their school to visit, or reconnect with their favorite teacher at homecoming. Decades immediately dissolve away. They talk and laugh as much about the tough situations as they do the wins. It turns out that the old memories make a bigger impression on us than the championships and test scores that everyone stressed over every year.

The words that live on in our students' hearts and minds aren't the lessons that are *taught*, they are the ones that are *caught*. That's the tricky part about unofficial communication. We don't remember the press releases, lecture notes, and announcements. It's the words in between, off-the-cuff, late at night, in a fast-food restaurant, that stick with us for a lifetime.

And with Coach Wood, a lot of it stuck. I actually tried *The Look* in my first year as a coach. It didn't work. But Coach Wood's style of employing humor and building relationships did. I used his old joke about the outfielder who missed a fly ball because he couldn't see them when they reached a height of ninety feet. My players laughed and, to my surprise, listened to my coaching on fly ball communication. But that same sense of humor was indispensable in my algebra classroom. His style of teaching helped me start the process of finding my own.

Coach Wood isn't with us anymore, but his influence lives on to impact my students. We hear a lot about influencers in our social media driven world, but has an Instagram post ever stuck with you like that? The impact of our words is an underappreciated aspect of professional conduct because all our old educators still speak to us. They wouldn't let us slack off during sprints, or before that big test, and their voice is still there pushing us as an adult.

~

Like many, I received a rude awakening at my first college baseball practice. As I passed the foul pole to begin another lap, my new coach tried to get under my skin, *"What did Raleigh Wood ever teach you?"*

Little did he know, that was a perfect question to ask. I immediately thought to myself, *"A lot, actually."* It turns out I learned enough to become a coach myself, trying to impact the world just like Coach Wood impacted me. What a blessing it was to begin my journey as an educator with this powerful understanding of attitude's effect on communication. I will forever be thankful for his example.

Communicating Empathy

And then there is listening, perhaps the most underrated mode of them all. Does anyone listen anymore?

Of course they do. Just wait until the end of your next faculty meeting and you'll see it. When your principal closes with the obligatory *Any questions?* silence will immediately blanket the room as everyone strains to listen, praying no one takes the bait.

The conventional wisdom on listening—that no one does it—is wrong. We can hear each other just fine. It's doing the work to receive and understand what people say from their point of view, without criticism or judgment, that isn't happening. And why is that? Why are we so good at selective hearing, but so bad at the act of listening to improve understanding?

Lack of empathy. A closer look at the act of questioning explains why.

When a person asks a sincere question, they are communicating, too. Their question reveals two very important facts about themselves to anyone within earshot.

> Why are we so good at selective hearing, but so bad at the act of listening to improve understanding? Lack of empathy.

1. They don't understand something.
2. They publicly announce their confusion about that topic.

Consider the end of that faculty meeting again, with its call for questions and the awkward silence that follows. Not only would a questioner have to speak up to extend the meeting, thereby committing a cardinal sin, they must also make their self-diagnosed "stupidity" public knowledge. As a result, more often than not, they just hold on to it.

And then, if your administrator is truly sadistic, they'll throw in a caveat after they've presented some new, or particularly complex information. *"Seriously, there are no dumb questions."* As if that would coax a hesitant person to speak up.

How often does this scenario occur in our classrooms?

The faculty meeting is a fun illustration, but hardly the worst. When people feel afraid to ask sincere questions that might reveal their confusion, or true thoughts, it can paralyze any possible improvement in a classroom, a department meeting, or even an entire school district. This chilling effect on genuine curiosity keeps people from speaking up. So questioning, and therefore listening, is all about the environment.

Two important requirements must be met, though, before we can invite sincere questions or receive honest answers:

1. Is the environment for communication free from risk?
2. Can the speaker offer their input without fear of revealing their confusion?

It's important to note that we often use the word "environment" here, but this doesn't denote a location. What we are really talking about is a relationship that is conducive to communicating. Lending an ear that doesn't judge. Listening, or receiving someone's input with an appreciation for their point of view, communicates to the speaker that we value their input. When you feel that safety with a colleague, or with your teacher, you don't mind communicating your vulnerability to them.

In short, we need conversations to occur in schools where we are comfortable telling each other the truth. Listening is the only way to build a culture that encourages this deep commitment to improvement. Professionals listen to students, colleagues, and parents to gain understanding, not as a pause to fire back a reply.

I learned the value of this "environment" for communicating as a young assistant coach. In the midst of a tight ballgame that would determine the district championship, our head coach approached me during a break in the action. The setting was wild. We had just homered to tie the game. As our student section went berserk, the opposing team's coach called time to discuss strategy. That's when Jerry walked over to check my pitching chart, look down the bench, and ask a simple question.

"Who do you think we should put in to pitch the last inning?"

The physical environment couldn't have been less conducive to conversation, I could hardly hear him. But the relationship was right. I looked down the bench and talked through our options with my mentor. *"Kyle has the best stuff to get the middle of their lineup out, but he pitched three innings on Tuesday. Michael is rested and has a better fastball. He's not as experienced, but I think he could do it."*

Now, this may sound like a short, trivial interaction. But our team's chances of making the playoffs hung on this decision. Jerry had decades of coaching experience, had been in situations like this hundreds of times, and likely already knew which pitcher he wanted on the mound. Yet, he still wanted input from a young coach like me. He thought for a second, nodded his head and sent me down to the bullpen to watch both of them warm up.

"Let me know which one looks better."

Forget the outcome of the game. By now, I sure have. My mentor wanted input on a key decision from me. It was a short, honest interaction between two people whose relationship was built on a shared goal. Asked and answered. No big deal, right?

Hardly. In my mind, that question changed my status as a member of the coaching staff. Contributing input to the outcome of such a big game served as proof that my hard work was paying off. Jerry listened to my answer. My opinion was valued.

Listening to understand, instead of waiting for the next opportunity to reply, is the approach that deepens a relationship. Imagine the impact if we made phone calls to parents with this same curiosity:

"Good afternoon, Mrs. Sellers. This is Mrs. Bass, Johnny's reading teacher. Do you have a few minutes to talk? I noticed that Johnny has been very talkative in class this week and had a hard time paying attention. Have you noticed anything like this at home?"
The next part of the script is simple: LISTEN.

Listening is hard. It takes time. But it's an act of service that explains the difficulty behind our jobs. And it is the only way we will slowly build, or rebuild, lasting trust with our community. When we talk about the expertise involved in being an educator, and how hard our jobs are, we are referencing the act of listening. Seeking to understand, in today's social media-technology age, is the act of service that educators pledge to our stakeholders. It's a service that few others in our society will offer.

The trust that we so desperately seek to establish with our communities is built on each of us making dozens of phone calls like this each year, listening to the answer, and interacting with the parent to do what's best for the student. School districts can send out all the nice social media posts and official messages for years saying that we love our students and want to do what's best for them. But if we don't make a one-on-one connection that demonstrates this commitment, our official messaging rings hollow.

That's the power of listening. When done correctly, in consideration of another's point of view, it's a growth experience for us (Rogers and Farson, 1957).

How Does Bias Affect Communication?

But before we can build trust, we must be honest about our personal biases, which can undermine every other effort to communicate. If we believe it takes a village to raise a child, then we must assume that all the villagers are on the same page with respect to values. This is why communication exists on the same priority level as learning and safety.

If there is no alignment of values, the partnership falls apart. And if we don't understand our community's values, the strength of our instruction or the consistency of our safety protocols will not matter. You may have seen an illustration of the danger posed by this misalignment of values on social media. There are countless online accounts now that make a comfortable living reposting videos of "educators" who express a desire to promote their personally held values about sexuality, abortion, and other controversial political issues with their students. What an epic failure on their part.

The main offense isn't that these so-called educators said the quiet part out loud. The problem is that they purposely abused their influence over children to promote personal beliefs. Their subversive behavior, seeking to violate that precious trust, is then translated out to all educators. No wonder the relationship between parents and schools has frayed.

How we teach kids, and our approach of fairness toward all viewpoints, is under intense scrutiny because the *in loco parentis* concept, at least from a parent's point of view, means a partnership exists that includes some acceptance of beliefs. By giving an educator permission to stand in a parent's place the educator becomes a partner in raising their child. One popular idea that's been worn out in arguments about a school's role in raising kids goes something like this:

"Children should be taught how to think, and not what to think." (Mead, 1928, p. 246).

Margaret Mead gets credit for this lofty idea. She used it to conclude her first book, *Coming of Age in Samoa*. After living on a remote island in the Pacific for three years, she wrote it to document the sexual promiscuity of teenaged girls on the South Pacific island of Ta'u. The immortal quote summarized her belief that behavior and expectations are taught to kids and carry more weight than biological differences in creating a culture.

Contrasting the primitive culture of Samoa against Roaring 20's American society, with all its contradictions, was Dr. Mead's way of highlighting the dangerous influence of majority beliefs, however wrong they may be, on a society. Her take on early 20th century child-rearing was simple: Parents and society used to brainwash behavior and biases into their kids, which served as a basis for the messed-up culture of the day.

Sound familiar?

But Margaret Mead, famed anthropologist that she was, had not raised any children of her own at the time her important work was printed. If she had, she would've understood that parenting is nothing if not a prolonged effort to make children think exactly the way you do. And if a parent feels that our actions as educators could get between those beliefs and their kid, problems are sure to follow.

A century later, Dr. Mead's timeless quote still resonates, and is a worthy goal for the education of children. But critics often assume that teachers can remove all bias from their classrooms as they work to teach kids to think objectively. And that's just not realistic.

The overwhelming majority of teachers who wade into America's culture war didn't choose education to make a lot of money or indoctrinate the next generation. They just long to help other peoples' kids grow up, graduate, and be successful. And yet, personal bias has become one of the biggest criticisms of educators. That's because we are human. Everyone is biased in some way. It's acknowledging that our biases exist that helps us neutralize them as stumbling blocks. Understanding the destructive nature of personal bias is imperative to maintaining our credibility.

Years ago, I held a political discussion in my U.S. History class that illustrates how difficult it is to manage bias in the classroom, even when you go to great lengths to remove it. Our study on yellow journalism, a sensational style of writing where newspaper editors would twist events to make a splash and sell more newspapers, went off the rails when my students interjected their own opinions into a heated topic.

My lesson hinged on attribution of the 1898 explosion of the battleship *U.S.S. Maine* in Havana, Cuba, which killed hundreds of American sailors. The front pages of American newspapers were plastered with pictures, drawings, and diagrams pointing to a Spanish mine as the cause. But that story was fiction.

To illustrate this common practice of the news media stretching the truth based on their biases, I nearly started World War III in my classroom by showing stories that were widely circulated after the tragic death of Trayvon Martin, a teenager who was killed in a high-profile shooting. The information I presented was accurate. Several news outlets literally made-up information to fuel more outrage at the tragedy and garner more views.

But I completely stepped in it by picking such a hot-button topic without first laying the proper ground rules. There was serious disagreement between some of my students. Instead of discussing my illustration of the blatant inaccuracy of the news media, my students spent a great deal of time discussing the motivations behind the shooting. It was an epic failure on my part. I was forced to stop all discussion and restart the lesson. When the bell rang an hour later, they understood my point. But not before my heart rate, and their volume level, went through the ceiling.

Learning from my mistakes could help your students. Here are some priorities to remember if students start buzzing about a breaking news event:

Expect students to be curious. Students will want to know information about big current events. They will look to their teachers to make sense of them. Civic participation is something we want our students to be engaged in, so don't immediately shy away from hot button topics. If that discussion starts, be sure to maintain the floor.

Control the discussion. You are the chairman of your classroom. Don't let students talk over or at each other. It's OK for them to express opinions about an event, even if they aren't all that informed. It's not OK for them to inject incorrect facts or demean anyone. If you feel that you are losing control of the discussion, end it immediately. Students are often too impulsive in expressing their opinions. When that happens, a student who disagrees will impulsively respond, usually louder, in reply. The situation devolves from there. This can't happen. Set ground rules before any discussion takes place.

The Ground Rules. Our students must be taught how to listen first, and then look for connections. In humanities courses, we should be teaching our students how to disagree. It's important for students to learn that shouting down a viewpoint they disagree with, which is common in political debate these days, is unacceptable. And it's important for parents to know that we, as educators, will not put our foot on the scale when controversial topics come up in our classrooms. Get students to follow these rules in a controversial classroom discussion and you just made the world a little bit safer for freedom of speech:

> Respect classmate's freedom to speak.
> Listen to the viewpoint and ask clarifying questions.
> Point out differences AND common ground.
> Respect a classmate's freedom to disagree.

Forget personal opinions during the discussion. Easy to say, hard to do. You can't moderate a discussion while pulling for one side. Don't expect teenagers to do any better than the dumpster fire of data that adults post in your own news feed. If this idea of bias seems like an over-exaggeration to you, then you may have too much buy-in to be impartial. Don't conduct this discussion in your classroom. You have a right to your own opinions, but not to teach your opinions to your students. Margaret Mead's goal for society is a worthy effort for a classroom discussion on controversial issues. From our positions of trust, we should teach students to think for themselves, even when that leads them to disagree with us.

Stick to the facts. Students bring their personal impression of events with them to school. They will bring biases from their parents with them as well. Some incidents will take years for our country to process. Very few classroom discussions will speed up that healing process. But a discussion based on incorrect facts can make the situation worse.

Dispel fake news. It is also likely that students may bring incorrect facts to a discussion. This is where original source material and first-person accounts are invaluable. And be careful with "news" articles. A great deal of the stories reported by major news companies as fact aren't any more accurate than William Randolph Hearst's diagram of the Spanish mine that sank the *Maine*.

Play devil's advocate. To properly control discussion, you need to read enough about the events before students arrive so that you understand both sides of the issue. A teacher that recognizes their bias goes to great lengths to make points from either side of an issue. You will know you've done it correctly if students can't tell which political side you agree with.

Remember the event's relevance to your content. Social studies classrooms, or language arts, are ideal settings for discussions about political or controversial issues. If you happen to be a political junkie, but teach some other content, political discussions just aren't necessary or even appropriate. It is certainly OK for a brief discussion about a big event to take place, but the further your curriculum is from social events, the quicker the discussion should be steered back to the current lesson.

Days when controversial events occur are when we really earn our money. We want our country to be a place where we can disagree, debate the issues, and come to a conclusion that benefits as many people as possible. Majority rule is part of that process, but our government has so many checks and balances built in, that minority opinions have a say. Free speech, that allows for opposing viewpoints, is what keeps the American ideal alive. Helping students understand the responsible use of it is where Margaret Mead's timeless idea came from.

We want to encourage our students to analyze these situations from both sides, which means a healthy dose of empathy can help these discussions tremendously. But we will have to model empathy for most students. With any luck, some of the kids in your room will take it with them to Washington, D.C., someday.

Guiding Principles of Professionalism for Communication

Communication is a fundamental aspect of an educator's contribution to the culture of learning because it is the means by which we do our work. But it is also the avenue where most of the breakdowns occur.

As we've already established, communication carries the most expectations for professional conduct. Student safety is intertwined with communication. We've already discussed unmonitored, one-on-one communication between an educator and a student, but it is so dangerous, it bears repeating. It cannot occur through any medium. This is a dangerous situation and should be reported immediately, even if it occurs by accident.

Regardless of your role, whether teacher or administrator, put serious thought into your expectations before beginning any endeavor. Communicate those expectations as clearly as possible. Then, follow through on what you said you would do.

Social Media Guidelines for Educators. We shouldn't expect perfection when it comes to communication. But participating on social media almost requires it. The same issues that plague our students at every turn can haunt educators as well.

While we all enjoy the basic right to free speech, we are not absolved from its consequences. Make a controversial post, and you've etched a thought into stone. Go ahead and delete it. Doesn't matter. What happens online stays online, unfortunately. Odds are good that the screenshot will land in a school board member's inbox before your head hits the pillow tonight.

Like one of my mentors explained, social media is an area where we can learn from the bad examples. There are many so-called educators who've taken to social media to not only exercise their freedom of speech, but to profess their desire to purposely put their foot on the scale regarding some pretty heavy adult topics, such as gender identification, sexual conduct, and controversial political beliefs. Exercising their free speech in this way doesn't just harm their individual reputations, it spreads out across our entire profession.

Social media posts are generally harmless, right up until a post crosses the line. If you have any questions about where that line is, it's located right where you stand on your personal biases. And a post that promotes a bias that goes against the sentiment of even one family can have dangerous consequences for school community trust. Love your freedom of speech? Enjoy responsibly.

It takes some serious self-discipline to master this key method for building trust. But taking communication seriously, focusing on your speech, actions, and attitude, and listening to people with the intention of understanding their viewpoint will be a difference maker in building a stronger culture at your school.

~

It is evident in this chapter that I learned from some wonderful mentors in my journey through this profession. Undoubtedly, my lessons will remind you of individuals from your own past who understood the impact of their words and left you better off because of it. If you're looking for a starting point in improving communication, think small. Start with these three steps:

+ In official communication, be thorough. Details always matter, and documented facts always speak the loudest in any meeting.
+ In unofficial communication, be gracious. If a student puts you on the spot with their attitude, begging for a confrontation, take a step back. Be the adult in the room and help them detach from the situation. And, it might also be time for them to discuss the issue with an administrator.
+ For listening, be the ear that others need. Offer help and build that environment that encourages honesty. True listening is leadership.

It's possible—even likely at times—that the gravity of this job with its stacks of to-do lists regarding instruction, learning, safety, and communication, might grind you down. If you are at a point where you need a break, that's what you'll get in the next chapter, when we talk about how professionals find balance in their work.

CHAPTER 7

Balance

"*EW...MEW...MEW*" *A seagull startled Rebecca out of a brief nap. Lying under the sun, unbothered during this girls' trip was just what the doctor ordered. Now that school and her kids' sports were over, it was a relief to spend a few days with her feet in the sand. The biggest decision this week was where to eat dinner.*

As she reached for her drink, a Frisbee landed close by, spitting sand across her legs. A worried mother's loud voice immediately interrupted Rebecca's solitude. "Tommy, be careful with that toy!"

The kid ran over, picked it up, and sent it flying back across to his big brother. Rebecca's heart raced for a second, until she confirmed that this wasn't the same Tommy from her class this past school year. Her mind immediately went back to a day just before spring break, when her Tommy had disrupted class in an unusual manner. A smile inched across her face at the thought.

After passing out a unit test that day, she gave her standard directions for students to take their time and read each problem carefully. That's when Tommy stood up and made an odd announcement to her 4th grade math class.

"I'm not going to take this test, Miss Hawkins! You didn't teach us how to work these problems!"

A Balanced Approach to Communication

Teaching is a balancing act. When little Tommy stands up and announces to twenty-five of his classmates that you didn't teach any of the information on his test, there are a million possible responses to his insolence. A reply that's too harsh risks worsening the problem. Too lenient, and you risk a repeat offense before anyone makes it to the word problems at the end.

How can you answer little Tommy when he puts you on the spot like this, and keep the class focused?

If you're looking for a rule to follow when reacting to these situations, there isn't one. But a hundred times a day, teachers are faced with decisions that call for just the right response. Immediately. No time to ask for help. The tool that aids an educator in these interactions is equal parts communication, attitude, and wisdom. Let's call it balance.

So, you scrap the first fifty responses that enter your mind because you need to keep your job. Then, as a consummate professional would, you strike just the right tone in response. Situations like these, putting a teacher on the spot in front of large groups of people, perfectly illustrates the art of teaching.

The concept of balance has to be one of the most confusing and stressful aspects of teaching. And, ironically enough, the more stressful the situation, the more balance is required. If you've ever experienced a misstep regarding professional conduct (spoiler alert: most everyone has at some point), you understand the mystery behind this puzzling feature of human interaction. Experience factors heavily into maintaining balance. It's how we learn not to take an issue too far.

Making judgment calls on the fly that involve curriculum, supervision, classroom management, instruction, people skills, safety concerns, patience, self-discipline, assessment, high expectations, communication, dedication to colleagues, testing guidelines, purpose, a sense of humor, customer service, and understanding with a professional response is a lot. And these issues aren't just present every day; they are subject to arise in every single interaction.

The future of our country depends on who will answer the call to serve as an educator. When one person makes that commitment, one small, unsuspecting corner of the world hits the lottery. But the cost of that decision is high. The stress and strain of having to make just the right decision, at just the right time, repeated multiple times a day, is one of those unwritten parts of the job description that wears people down.

In fulfilling this call, educators essentially devote their livelihoods as an act of service, distinguishing us from nearly every other career field. People with the patience to serve the needs of a community and the expertise to provide a safe, effective learning environment for other people's kids is a rare commodity today. Our ability, and willingness, to juggle these challenges is why the field education called us.

> Our willingness, and ability, to juggle these challenges is why the field education called us.

And in so many of those interactions, we are required as professionals to strike the perfect balance. How in the world do we teach educators to improve snap decision making and disregard the stressors that weigh everyone down?

It begins by learning to manage the one constant in our field: change.

The Force Working Against Balance

Whether it's a classroom disruption, a mad parent, new work expectations, or a job that won't stop growing, change is what makes achieving balance such a challenge. And change is unavoidable.

But even though an obstacle course often faces us just to get the day started, we persist. Because our mission is to serve. The efficiency and competence we've picked up along the way aid us. But eventually, some external force intervenes, or a law is passed, and the game changes again. Starting over in an area of expertise hits hard.

When frustrations inevitably arise, the harried educator is constantly urged to reconnect with their purpose—as though they had forgotten it. But diving headfirst into their purpose is exactly how this situation started. The daily work of service, combined with the well of patience required to manage this type of change, creates a paradox of sorts. Is it any wonder why we lose so many educators by year five?

Managing the change associated with being an educator is a necessity. Because change occurs so often in the school business, it's a constant in itself. Here are a few of the biggest change forces that create the complex work we face as educators:

Technology The change associated with technology is stunning. This is a particularly difficult aspect of education to grasp, for technology has provided a number of great tools to enhance the work of educating children. When properly implemented, these tools aid the journey to effectiveness and lead us to efficiency.

But, boy, is there a negative side to all that technology. Failing to grasp the many changes technology introduces to the classroom can leave an educator, and consequently their students, far behind. It can become quite a struggle to pull students into an engaging classroom discussion when they are conditioned to spending hours each day on social media. And the distractions student devices can provide, with their constant notifications, can make paying attention to a lesson nearly impossible. I could continue, but this isn't a book about technology—and I'll leave it up to you to figure out if I used an artificial intelligence language model to generate this portion of the chapter.

For educators to manage this aspect of change, we must set the environment for the proper use of devices on day one and stick to it.

School level policies are only as good as the consistency of the educators who work in the school. Faculty-level discussions should focus on what is appropriate in all classrooms, and then be boiled down into a manageable set of expectations that every teacher can apply to their classrooms.

The Generation Gap We've already established the value of connecting with colleagues. But assuming that will just happen once you get people in the same room is the height of naivety. The career structure for educators in most states requires a commitment of thirty years to receive full retirement benefits. So, the makeup of any faculty will likely contain an age range of nearly forty years. Communication between these different generations can be really tough. Some people might prefer face-to-face conversation, while others prefer electronic communication. Some, literally no communication. The only thing they have in common: most everyone forgets to read their emails.

How a school disseminates its official messaging and schedule is another school-level conversation that administrators should facilitate. Getting everyone on the same page with respect to preferred modes of communication can prevent confusion and is a wonderful culture builder.

The Force that Brings Balance

As difficult as it can be to constantly navigate the many changes facing educators, we must accept not only the inevitability of change, but also the positive aspects of it as well. It doesn't take a deep dive into the history of American education to see the benefits of change. How else would improvement occur? There are plenty of stark examples that illustrate the value of change. Let's look at a recent one.

Consider a 1:1 school device policy and think about the change in classroom norms when these devices were first introduced. Standing at the front of the classroom to monitor students and teach was the standard that worked (more or less) for a long time before this miraculous influx of technology. But stay at the front of the room for the whole period, while students work silently on their devices, and you may have the quietest, but also the most unproductive classroom ever.

The introduction of technology on this scale made teacher movement a must for effective instruction while students use devices at their desks. But this wonderful change created a physical demand on the teacher that wasn't there before. The stool/podium combo I grew up expecting in a classroom gave way to comfortable shoes, and teacher desks at the back of the room. The outcome of this change in teacher behavior? Students who spend more time on task when given an assignment to complete on their school device, because they can't tell when the teacher, positioned behind them, is looking at their screen

Change is a paradox. It hurts. At the same time, it helps. And the biggest force for change confronts us every single moment of the day: the students we serve.

Students Technology and the generation gap team up as change agents in the form of our students. Their fad-crazed personalities are what make teaching simultaneously challenging and rewarding. But regardless of the trend du jour, there are still some principles that do not change with students. We've already discussed the value of communicating your purpose to them.

But as generations pass, one constant remains: deep down, students crave structure. They want a teacher who they can depend on to lead them. Respect, not likability, is a student's measure of a good teacher, even if they won't admit it publicly. You've got to feel good about that aspect of change, even if it dramatically increases your step count.

Personal Balance

It's appropriate that I'm writing this section in the early morning hours, while seated in a comfortable chair with my feet propped up. My cat,

Riley, is purring in my lap. A steaming mug of coffee sits next to an old Dietz lantern that was converted into an electric lamp. Outside, dawn is slowly revealing a cold rain. I'm trying my hardest to relax, but stress continues to overwhelm. Writing serves as a therapy of sorts for me. But pre-registration for next year is beginning. Student discipline has begun its yearly climb. Everyone is a bit on edge. It is January 2024.

If the thought of wintertime at the end of my self-care scene raised your heart rate a few beats, I understand why. Winter can be a scary time for many educators, far and away the hardest stretch of the school year. We often eclipse the one-hundred-day mark and find ourselves frustrated and stressed, nerves and bodies frayed. Winter is the season when we realize the danger of being consumed by our calling. If you're in a season of life where fending off a panic attack is a routine occurrence, *self-care* might be your only alternative to *urgent care* at a hospital.

> If you're in a season of life where fending off a panic attack is a routine occurrence, self-care might be the only alternative to urgent care.

This oppressive feeling comes from serving students, the community, and our own families' needs at the expense of our own. Sanity suffers, because the technological advances that allow us to work while we are at home can seem like punishment. The result? Every year we reach this portion of the calendar completely drained. Splitting a finite amount of time between two seemingly infinite needs, work and family, will do that to you.

But the seasons of life have a way of making rest elusive. The young assistant coach, whose timeclock approaches seventy hours a week, seemingly living on campus, lives with constant physical exhaustion. But there is no time for rest. She starts an eight-hour shift every day when the classroom door closes. Then she heads to the volleyball court.

Weekends are included.

This scenario repeats throughout the building. How does the English teacher grade all those essays? And what about the four students who missed yesterday's test? Two will come in early tomorrow, which means another hour on the phone with the other two sets of parents to schedule another makeup date.

We are all working the equivalent of two (or more) full-time jobs. And it always seems to catch up to us during the winter months.

Rest, the first component of self-care, is what we long for. And it can actually be achieved quickly. Unfortunately, most self-care conversations stop there. But rest is just the first of three critical components of true self care. Recharging and refreshment deserve just as much emphasis. True self-care is accomplished through reconnection. With the people that are closest to us, and with the reasons why we teach.

The third term of a school year always pushes educators toward the self-care aisle of the bookstore because it's the season we are most in need. Balance is usually an afterthought when we approach February. Why is that? Well, discipline rates typically hit their peak between winter break and spring break (Darling-Hammond, et. al, 2023).

But most of the available reading on self-care is incomplete. Doing nothing isn't a cure to what ails us when the grind hits its hardest phase. It never fails, when I follow some deep thinker's advice to prop my slippered feet up on the hearth and take a break with a good book and a cup of coffee, the stressors are always still there when I finish. But the problems are even bigger now because I feel guilty for wasting time relaxing. All I did was get away for a minute. This pseudo-remedy is really just escapism masked as self-care, which makes the struggle worse and can even create a downward spiral.

Health is the goal of self-care. And true self-care meets our mental, physical, and spiritual needs. Personally, my connection with spirituality comes from my faith in God. While there are many avenues available in this pursuit, I'm going to offer some principles here that have sustained me through some difficult personal times. I hope they can provide spiritual nourishment for you as well. Let's begin by considering some timeless wisdom from the book of Proverbs:

> *"A generous person will prosper; whoever refreshes*
> *others will be refreshed."*
> Proverbs 25:11 (NIV)

This short sentence towers over all other self-care literature. We could all benefit from spending a couple of months unpacking this one verse. If refreshment is our goal, we won't really get it from ourselves, or our devices. I tend to agree with the idea that scripture reads best when you think of it as a hyper-linked text. Go through it slowly enough, and every sentence you read is an extension of a previously stated truth.

And the more I think about Proverbs 25:11, considering the value of generosity and helping others, the more I'm reminded of my own true needs. These needs are summarized even better in this passage from the book of Deuteronomy.

> *"Man does not live by bread alone."*
> Deuteronomy 8:3 (NIV)

This is a shorter verse that says even more. Fulfilling our hunger and physical needs is an obvious requirement. But rest, or good food, two things that self-care gurus spend the most time on, won't complete us. I'm sorry to bear bad news, but the next holiday won't be enough either.

It sounds counterintuitive, but rest, by itself, won't solve our exhaustion problem. There is a good kind of tired. A two-mile walk with the kids, devices locked in the car, is one way to reach it. And there is a bad kind of rest. Waking up from a nap and immediately dreading some impending future event isn't restful at all. Searching for happiness and quiet—the pop-culture-approved version of self-care—can rob us of joy and peace. And that isn't caring for ourselves at all.

We can all identify an elephant in our room, but all the rest in the world won't remove it. Our best self-care might be to tackle it, instead of taking a nap. But some of those burdens aren't going anywhere, no matter what we do. Reconnecting with those closest to us, with our friends, our family, and with our faith, remain the best ways for making it through.

As the next holiday approaches, it's important to remember that rest alone won't refresh. Of course it's important, but it's not the only priority. Solomon didn't say he who rests will be refreshed. So, take a breather, then prepare to serve again. With any luck, we won't be begging for another vacation on the Monday we return to work.

~

Major-league stressors like student needs, tight schedules, anxiety, family needs, classroom discipline, testing, and accountability demands aren't going anywhere. Practicing self-care won't make these mountains melt away, but it can definitely equip us to climb them.

Self-care is a vital component of personal balance, so it must be considered an equally important requirement for educator professionalism. The connection is simple. Fulfilling your life's purpose as an educator is a blessing. Bogging down in stress, anxiety, and guilt because you are spread too thin to serve others can make it a curse.

How can a teacher meet basic student needs if they haven't met their own? Answering the following questions can help you locate areas that need attention so you can stay sharp, even on days when you just aren't feeling it. If you can answer "yes," go on to the next question. This starts you down a healthy path to achieving personal balance:

Am I eating right?
Am I getting enough sleep?
Am I getting enough exercise?
Am I in conflict with anyone?
Do I need to refocus my faith?

Physical issues can start a downward spiral, accelerating the stress, anxiety, and depression you feel. But we can't let that take our focus off mental and spiritual health. If time is an issue, consider waking up 15-20 minutes earlier every day for some reading or meditation time. Morning quiet time is without a doubt the most underrated shortcut to mental balance in the day. Think about it: those few minutes of sleep will be long forgotten at 2:00 in the afternoon. You're already tired then anyway.

A sixth suggestion: Working in the isolation of a classroom makes it imperative that we intentionally interact with others. Widen your circle. Stay positive. The self-talk we hear from ourselves can be self-care, or self-defeating. Share your problems. Talk things out and build each other up. The interaction is beneficial for you and your colleague. Refresh others, and you will in turn be refreshed.

There is a reason that Richard Elmore's quote about the dangers of isolation is so appropriate for educators. It follows this same principle. Isolation prevents improvement, but it also prevents interaction. If we don't help our colleagues stay refreshed, we are also hurting ourselves. And on some days, those colleagues aren't just necessary refreshment; we often need them just to survive.

Another suggestion: When requests for your time bog you down and deadlines seem to crowd everything out, take a break from social media. It steals hours of our time that could be spent on our families, or in productive work. Doom scrolling is just another version of escapism. And it's as unhealthy as it sounds.

Instituting stronger personal boundaries is another step to finding balance. Educators often get advised to say "No" more often to become more productive at work. This isn't a call to be grumpy, or disagreeable, though. It's a suggestion to better organize our daily schedules. Plan breaks or family activities in advance. Build them into your calendar first. Then stick to them when you receive those last-minute requests for your time. Declining one of those extra requests might save you some sanity.

And here's one final suggestion: If these tips don't offer relief, it could be time for some professional help. Employee assistance programs have thankfully become a viable, convenient option for educators. The stigma associated with professional mental health support is thankfully melting away. Take advantage of this wonderful resource.

Self-care isn't about being selfish or putting yourself first. And it's not an indulgence to escape from your problems. It's confronting change, or student needs, with an attitude of confidence. Self-care, which allows us to maintain that confidence, is how we strengthen ourselves so we can continue to serve others.

Classroom Management, Another Obstacle to Balance

Is there a task that has more impact on a teacher's mental state than classroom management? All the self-care in the world won't overcome the dread that hits on a Sunday evening when we face an upcoming week of dealing with unruly students. Not only is bad student behavior an extreme stressor for teachers, but the added guilt from feeling as though you are responsible for allowing that bad behavior makes it twice as bad.

We've touched on some principles of communication that are worth revisiting here. Communicating classroom expectations on the first day of school can be done a million different ways. Some teachers choose the democratic method of developing classroom rules and procedures collaboratively, and some hand them out like a benevolent dictator. How these procedures are generated isn't nearly as important, though, as the consistency that follows. All the rules in the world can't overcome inconsistent application. It's the follow through that makes all the difference.

Earlier in this chapter, we discussed the value of accepting change. But when it comes to classroom management, students need a North Star to keep them on track. This is where the rubber meets the road of maintaining order in a classroom. Our reaction to all those little change agents in front of us needs to be predictable. That's how we provide our students structure.

Classroom management is tough for teachers, though, because it's really self-management. Unfortunately, there is only one person in the classroom whose behavior you can control: your own. So, managing a classroom full of students really comes down to five simple actions that a teacher takes each day:

+ Communicate procedures and consequences on Day 1.
+ Immediately begin observing for undesired behaviors.
+ Respond to those behaviors, or any other interruption, immediately and in the manner that was communicated in #1.
+ Don't take little Tommy's outburst personally. He's just a kid!
+ Go back to #1 and start over tomorrow.

Like we've said before, these tenets are simple, but not easy. The consequences a teacher spells out on day one absolutely must be followed to the letter. If the steps for addressing poor behavior call for a warning, then warn them. Once. And if the next step calls for something different, don't warn that student anymore. Go up the ladder to some higher level. Warnings only work once. When a student receives multiple warnings, they hear: *"I'm not going to hold you to the expectation I set."*

Guess what type of behavior you will see in response?

It's hard to overstate the importance of working through these procedures in a deliberate manner early on in a school year. For the first three weeks of school, behavior should be as much a priority in your lesson plans as any content objectives. Teach them how you want them to act.

It's also hard to overstate the importance of consistency to these procedures. Consistency, which implies an ability to repeat a desired behavior over a long period of time, is best achieved by a short-term mindset. If a teacher is devoted to improving classroom management, it can only be done one day at a time.

On the first day of school, follow the lesson plan with a minute-by-minute focus on student compliance with classroom procedures. If there is a particular aspect of teaching that you struggle to control, like group work, put those expectations out early and do some group work on the first day of school. For those first few days, even the most disruptive students in the school are compliant. Teach your content but watch their behavior like a hawk. Any slight misstep, or interruption to your plan should be addressed, according to your preset consequences. Immediately. Then, pick back up with the plan and keep on moving.

On the second day of school, we progress to the next appropriate spot in our lesson plans, but we start back at square one on behavior, continuing to watch them closely and addressing any missteps appropriately. Classroom management is best accomplished one day at a time. Keep this focus going day-by-day and you will eventually look up and realize it's October and class is running smoothly. That's consistency.

Following through on appropriate, predetermined, and over-communicated consequences, when the situation calls for it, is the work of a good classroom manager. And the end result is students who learn more, and a teacher who enjoys a bit more mental balance.

~

"I can't take this test, Miss Hawkins! You didn't teach us how to work these problems!"

Thinking back on that day, Rebecca could laugh now. Her heart had raced, turning her face red. But her response had diffused the boy's outburst of anger perfectly.

"Perhaps you missed our study guide yesterday, Tommy?"

He stomped his foot and immediately sat down.

Sitting on the beach, she couldn't keep her mind from drifting back to that moment. And as she replayed that scene in her mind, she began to rework the study guide for that unit on percentages.

"Maybe I could change up that study guide a little bit…" she wondered.

Guiding Principles for Seeking Balance

The concept of balance fits into an educators' contribution to the culture of learning by helping them move from surviving to thriving, because the school-year cycle, coupled with life at home, can be ruthless. But for educators who can maintain some semblance of balance through it all, that tough calendar can also be a comfort. The refreshed mind of a balanced educator always finds a way to turn back to reflection, which engages us back into the meaningful work of equipping our students for achievement.

Classroom management is a perfect example of how the concept of balance permeates everything an educator does in a school. My little essay on classroom management a few pages back stressed the simplicity of a teacher's actions. But in the real world, it can take years to hone these skills to perfection. If your experience was anything like mine, you had significant classroom management issues before Labor Day of your first year. Then the snowball only grew bigger as the year moved on. It seemed impossible at times.

Bruised after a tough first year, I entered year number two with a resolve to nip those problems in the bud. As a result, I ran a classroom like Ivan the Terrible, overcorrecting for all my first-year errors. By year three, I began to understand the balance required to respond to the little Tommy's of the world.

Miles Davis is credited with explaining this trial-and-error growth process well. His definition is, naturally, quite smooth:

Man, sometimes it takes you a long time to sound like yourself.

It's comforting to know that Mr. Davis, in all his brilliance, had to struggle to find his way. Perhaps he was a teacher too. Because for most of us mortals, a few years of trial and error begins to yield a smoothly-running classroom. Through those three years, I learned some valuable lessons on classroom management the hard way:

+ Never raise your voice. If they can't hear you, lower it.
+ Never argue. If you do, you just gave them all the bargaining power in a negotiation that shouldn't be taking place.
+ Friendship and respect are inversely proportional when applied to students and their teachers.
+ Never show favoritism.

There are no official guidelines for seeking balance as an educator. But the concept of balance is the aspect of educator conduct that makes professionalism so hard to achieve and to define. Maintaining balance might not be spelled out in the job description, but employing the self-discipline to achieve it is the difference between fulfilling your calling and suffering through a job.

There is one final example from scripture that applies well to this concept of balance. It's a warning from scripture that, oddly enough, gives me hope for the outlook of our profession:

"Not many of you should become teachers…because you know that we who teach will be judged more strictly."
James 3:1 (NIV)

The context is obviously different, but the message to educators today is almost identical. The high standard that communities hold for their educators implies a great respect for our positions and the work we do every day. But this final verse, warning about the dangers of sitting in a position of judgment, translates pretty clearly to our position of trust over a community's young people.

Get ready. You will be tested.

The responsibility of leading students and parents is an awesome one. When we assumed our positions, we took on the role of expert in some small area of content. How we communicate that content, relate to people, respond to the demands of the job, and judge the situations placed before us, places us on a pedestal in the community. This calling to service is the work for which we were chosen. Answering that call often requires a balancing act of wisdom and patience.

Seeking balance is a transition for us in our effort to define professionalism. Focusing on teaching and learning, school safety, and communication are all requirements of the job that are placed on us by the school district. The concept of balance is a completely different avenue of professionalism, because it looks at our ability to internalize this mission and sustain ourselves for the long haul.

Building trust within a school community asks a lot of educators. Accepting the inevitable changes that affect that work, while remaining physically and mentally healthy is also a necessity. The word "balance" might not show up in the job description either, but achieving it is a requirement for meeting all those challenges consistently.

Our final aspect of educator conduct is an outgrowth of this concept of balance and serves as the final piece of the puzzle in defining professional educator conduct. It also defines our role in a school's culture. And it is huge. The final component of building trust is our personal morale.

CHAPTER 8

Morale

Darius received a life-changing lesson on morale at a professional development conference early in his career. Morale wasn't the topic of the day, though. As a first-year teacher, he was there to learn about classroom management. The morning session offered plenty of good strategies, and he'd filled a couple of pages full of notes. But the conversation at lunch, with a semi-retired teacher, was unforgettable.

Being the only person from his school, Darius was surrounded by new faces. The young music teacher waited in line after the morning session was dismissed, chose a to-go box, and found an empty table. Another teacher soon joined him. "Hi, I'm Karen. I've taught freshman English language arts for the past thirty years, and I'm not sure I believe a word they've said all morning."

Darius wasn't sure how to respond. "Hi. My name's Darius and I teach music."

With the formalities out of the way, they were free to share their thoughts on the one thing they had in common, the morning session. Or, at least Karen was. She dominated the conversation.

"I'm not sure why we have to relearn everything so often. And you're a music teacher, I'm sure none of this even applies to you. What a waste!

It seems like lesson planning shouldn't have to be so complicated. Just go to the next chapter in the textbook. Why should I have to create a dog-and-pony show just to make my principal happy? And I'm supposed to believe my lesson plan will control my students? Hah! Rules are what they need. I mean, are worksheets really so bad?" she wondered aloud.

After a few bites, she continued. "And my principal. Ha! He hates me. That guy has successfully alienated me from the entire faculty. He is such a poor leader. Pleasing all the parents and coaches is his only priority. You know, he's the reason I'm here today. Told me I needed to take advantage of this training."

"I'd like to thank him in person." Darius thought to himself.

It was at this point that Karen introduced him to a new term. "You could probably guess by now, but teacher morale at my school is terrible."

Darius thought about that for a second and decided to change topics. "Well, this is my first year teaching. So, a lot of this is new to me. Fortunately, I'm engaged to be marri--"

"Oh, how exciting!" She interrupted and took off again. "I love my husband a lot more now that I don't see him as much. We divorced five years ago. And our children, boy are they stressful sometimes. You know, kids these days just don't listen anymore. It seems like every single kid on my roster this year is disrespectful. They don't turn in their work. They don't pay attention. You know, last week I gave them a thirty-question study guide, and then on the next day changed the title at top to "Test." You know how many of them failed it? TWENTY! Can you believe that?"

At this point, all Darius could do was check his watch. Surely the afternoon session would begin soon. "Maybe you could try challenging them more next time?"

Karen seemed offended by his question. "Listen, honey, you can believe that kind of fantasy if you want to. But there's no need to try and impress me. Thirty years ago I sounded just like you, but I know better now. You just wait. They'll wear you down, too."

Fortunately, lunch was ending. But the rant was not. As they finished up their lunches, Karen revealed her true thoughts. "You know, as bad as things are in the world today, I would not want to have children if I were your age."

Who's Responsible for Morale?

Morale is a huge component of school culture. Leaders who ignore it do so at their own peril. But is teacher morale totally on the principal? Google "teacher morale" and you'll instantly receive a hundred blog posts that solve the problem and boil the solution down to five neat bullet points. They make it sound so easy. And yet, morale is still one of the biggest barriers to a strong culture in many schools.

It's safe to say that morale has always been a touchy issue for educators. But it seems as though the issue today is deeper. Search "teacher morale" on social media and you will see teachers' unguarded thoughts about the daily grind of serving as an educator. Those posts paint a grim picture.

We've already discussed the fact that change factors are possibly the biggest stressors of our job. But the conversation on educator morale centers around the way this job changes us. The turnover in our society moves trends so quickly, it's hard to keep up.

And while embracing change may be an inevitable consequence of our calling, failing to embrace it might be even worse. The recruiting billboard for education sells graduates on the opportunity for impact. *"Change the world,"* they told us in college. But it's easy to miss the fine print when you're a young college student. Taking on this job will probably change you, too. Spending decades in the same classroom, while thousands of kids cycle through, has a way of affecting you. If you haven't figured it out yet, change is built into the system.

Most teachers start their careers in their early 20's, and before the first week ends, the old hats mistake them for a student. I wore a tie on

my first day and the lunch lady still wanted my number before giving me a square of pizza.

But pretty soon, they have to research what their students are talking about to stay current. Then, after a few more years, they have to research what their newly-hired coworkers are talking about just to stay up to date. By this time, the education industry has churned out a cycle or two of new ideas, informing teachers that their dozen or more years of experience are actually just ineffective practices. Then, the education bureaucracy latches on to them and mandates wholesale change. If they're not careful, teachers can look up and realize they are approaching twenty years of experience, don't know anyone they work with, and are told they need to start over from scratch.

Educators can experience an infinite number of scenarios along the way that can cause enthusiasm to slide. When that happens, a like-minded individual can help turn that frustration into negativity. This is how low morale can seep into even the strongest cultures.

None of those experts on morale ever talk about the fact that misery loves company. According to them, it is always the boss's (or some other outside factor's) fault. These disgruntled educators don't take advantage of the ready-made network within their faculty, so their isolation leads them to think their opinions speak for the group. And as they continue to broadcast complaints, some of them stick; their neighbor experiences a few bad days in a row, and pretty soon the negative talk becomes a self-fulfilling prophecy. This negativity trap can quickly spread, and absolutely kill a culture.

Sour attitudes can be found anywhere. In the conversation on morale, that's a tale as old as time. But sour situations, and mistakes, occur all the time, too. Change can certainly contribute to a person's low morale, but it isn't the only reason for it. I've known people who had good reason to be mad about a decision made over their heads, a negative performance report, or a hiring decision that didn't go their way. You have, too.

And if some big, bad event like that doesn't happen, there are always plenty of other negatives to be found in a job that requires acts of service on an hourly basis. Just ask a nurse, they see it all the time. But, please, don't start looking for the negatives. They'll find you on their own soon enough.

Grumpy Guy: Morale here sucks.
Neighbor: Yeah!

So, who's responsible for morale in a school? The leaders are. And that's where the rub comes in when educators discuss morale. We know who the leaders are. We've already identified them. That's us. Personal morale is *every professional's* responsibility.

Think about the expectations that parents have for us when they drop their children off at school every morning. Serving *in loco parentis*. If we are going to work in a manner that shows the school community that we are worthy of parents' trust, that we are ready to stand in their place as parents, it is imperative that we bring enthusiasm, confidence, and loyalty to work with us every day. All the expertise in teaching and learning, safety, communication, and mental balance will never overcome a terrible attitude.

Unfortunately, you might have experience with a colleague similar to Karen. When you take another look at her attitude, three distinct characteristics stand out that distinguish her morale as one of the lowest you may ever encounter. Let's break them down. If you're battling any of these forces at work, maybe a closer look can show you a way out of the woods.

The Danger of Negativity

The most obvious theme from Darius's eye-opening conversation was an overabundance of complaints. Every single issue Karen encountered at work was wrong. But it's important to note, negatives aren't an indictment on a school's culture. In fact, negatives are actually a key feature of all schools. Put enough people together in a confined space for 180 days and you can expect some problems.

> Negatives aren't an indictment on a school's culture. In fact, negatives are a key feature of all schools.

It's what educators do with the negative, once uncovered, that makes all the difference in the world. Our mindset in the face of problems is the single most important determinant of individual morale, and a grossly underrated aspect of professional conduct.

If you've spent more than five minutes as an educator, you might have dealt with a negative situation or two. Maybe it's students that don't study or bring little prerequisite knowledge to your class. Or parents who don't discipline their children. Or worse, an administrator who won't. And maybe it isn't a big picture negative at all. It could just be a request for a repair that was ignored.

Negativity, on full display in our opening scenario, is a completely different problem. Negativity is an ingrained attitude of pessimism that constantly seeks out problems, but never worries itself with solutions. Assigning blame is always the objective. Once found, problems are welcomed, because they serve as confirmation of poor management, bad students, weak parents, or all the above.

Educators who suffer from negativity save their biggest complaints when encouraged or directed to change the status quo. To them, every new encounter is just wrong. Instead of serving as an opportunity for improvement, change is instead an immovable obstacle. In the face of intractable problems, the status quo always looks preferable in the world of negativity.

At its heart, a negative mindset is a subconscious attempt to shirk responsibility. Consequently, cultures that allow negativity to exist are dangerous because they prevent educators from taking a hard look at problems and breaking them down to their root causes. It takes courage to do that kind of work, because at the root cause you will always find the most dangerous aspect of negativity and low morale: the truth.

Professionals who take responsibility for maintaining their own morale aren't afraid to tell people the truth when they find the source of a problem. And good school leaders who understand how to support their people aren't afraid to hear it either.

Negativity prevents improvement, which, ultimately, hurts students. When tough situations surface, negative educators survive by telling the higher ups what they want to hear in an effort to maintain the safety of the status quo. That's the danger of negativity to a school community.

Don't entertain it.

The Danger of Indifference

But before you storm into some poor administrator's office and deliver the truth with the blunt force of a sledgehammer, don't forget the other key feature of professional conduct that is equally vital in solving serious problems: Empathy.

You wouldn't think apathy would be a problem for educators, but when you consider the amount of separation that exists between the different divisions in a school district's organizational chart, indifference to people who serve in different roles is an obvious consequence.

It's not a stretch to imagine the potential divisions that could occur after Coach Smith's terrible Monday morning back in Chapter One. Mrs. Walker, a close colleague of Coach Smith, would likely be quite curious about the situation. But her position as a teacher would prohibit her from learning any details of the situation. Her curiosity could easily get the best of her and turn into a sour take on Dr. Burrell's handling of the incident. The rumor mill would likely run rampant, and her feelings about the incident would only get worse.

Teachers who stay isolated from each other are one way we damage morale. But the separation between the different levels within a school district is an even stronger form of isolation to break through. And the gulf between some of the positions in our school districts is quite large.

One of the first eye-opening lessons for any teacher who moves into administration is the amount of work that takes place at school every day about which they were previously unaware. Going back to our opener again, the impending investigation of Coach Smith's lapse in supervision is a good example. Dr. Burrell would spend entire days on this investigation talking to teachers, students, and parents, taking statements, reviewing security footage, reporting findings to central office, and coordinating with Human Resources along the way. Investigations can be slow, stressful work. And not a single detail can be revealed to the teachers who know Coach Smith as a trusted colleague.

This separation, solidified after spending years in a single position, can eventually occupy all of an educator's mental space and prevent them from considering what their colleagues know or experience on a daily basis. It also keeps large groups of educators in the dark about major decisions because most of this information is mandated by law to remain confidential.

Central office administrators undergo this transition again when they assume their positions. And as the years pass, they can suffer from the same separation that can affect school building administrators as well. Not only are they dealing with different issues at the district level, but quite often they deal with them from a different zip code.

This separation leads to an odd form of indifference for the important tasks that must take place within the different levels of a school system. From teachers who claim their principals have forgotten what it's like to teach. From principals who claim central office administrators have forgotten what it's like to be in a school building. And from everyone in the school community, claiming the superintendent has forgotten everyone.

It's important to be cognizant of the fact that everyone has a tough, though very different, role to play in the success of a school. And for the higher ups, it's important to remember that very few people you interact with will likely ever know the pressures and challenges associated with your position. But, they will all understand what it's like to serve under you. So, grace and empathy should be a key feature in how we handle the truth, interact with each other, and make decisions that affect those above, and below us, on the ladder. When looking downward on the organizational chart, this principle works at every level: superintendents to the entire school community; principals to teachers, parents and students; and teachers to students and parents.

We would all do well to employ more empathy in conversations with the higher ups and with those below us. There are likely many details about the negative currently occupying our thoughts that we either can't, or don't, know.

Truth is sometimes painful, but how it is delivered makes all the difference in the world. High-morale professionals don't shy away from the truth, but they know the importance of employing understanding and empathy when dealing with it.

The Nightmare of Helplessness

As difficult as it is to describe morale, this third aspect is even harder to confront. Chances are good that if you're reading a book to improve your professional conduct, you don't suffer from negativity. And it's likely that you already understand the importance of employing empathy in your daily interactions. But even though you might be an optimist who considers the viewpoint of others every time a contentious issue arises, you still might get crapped on every day at work. The environment is just toxic. You've done everything you know to do, given it your best shot, and it still sucks. The list of pros doesn't justify living like this.

Working in an environment where despair is a daily feeling is dangerous. A feeling of helplessness at work is where the conversation on low morale transitions into a conversation about health.

I've felt despair in conversations with colleagues before. I've felt it myself at times, too. Health problems, home life, all these outside factors—plus the rigors of the job—can just burn the fun out of it and feel like a weight that never lifts off your shoulders. This isn't a book to help you solve a despair problem with a few solid suggestions. If you feel as though you don't have a say, and it's been that way for a long time, work becomes a prison.

If the best description for your situation at work is despair, it is likely time to have a hard conversation with someone or just forgive them for a wrong that was committed. That may not be easy, but it's certainly better than holding it in for two decades. Becoming an educator may change all of us, but extended periods of bitterness can make a person unrecognizable.

If a hard conversation with the boss doesn't change the situation, and there's no good option for connecting with colleagues for support, a change in location may be the only solution to a feeling of helplessness at work.

Guiding Principles for Maintaining Personal Morale

School culture can often seem larger than life. So big that a single person cannot influence it. By now we should have exposed that belief as a myth. Morale is how the individual makes an impact on an entire culture. Discussions about professionalism don't usually include morale, but I have yet to come across an educator with a positive personal attitude towards their job that didn't also meet the professional responsibilities of their work with vigor. Unlike the principles of safety, or teaching and learning, there are no explicit professional guidelines for educators to follow in taking ownership of morale. But the unwritten rules are voluminous. Any educator who is serious about supporting the culture of learning at their school understands their responsibility for maintaining their own personal morale.

You can't have a positive culture without high levels of morale among the members of the culture. And you can't have high levels of morale without leadership—leadership that includes all professionals on staff. Is your school better because of your personal brand of leadership you bring each day? Is your school better because of your morale? That's the kind of reflection that helps fortify teacher morale (Kafele, 2019).

All the conversations in a school among the adults, good days and bad days added together, determine a culture. This makes morale the final piece of the puzzle in defining professional conduct, because it is the difference-maker in every single one of those interactions. And when those interactions trend downward, culture will suffer.

Weak cultures serve as a breeding ground for low morale because educators in these schools ignore problems. On the other hand, when negatives occur in strong cultures, they can quite often lead to impromptu speeches that serve as wonderful motivational quotes. You'll hear random people speak to them when they uncover a negative in the process of carrying out the mission: *"Hey, we don't do that here."*

The old saying "There is no I in a TEAM" exists for a reason. You can't participate on a team successfully by focusing on yourself. But when it comes to participating in a culture, self-reflection on attitude and finding your fit within the organization is a requirement. There might not be room for an I-person on a TEAM, but there is definitely a ME in a team's MORALE.

My morale affects my colleagues. So, as a professional, I must take responsibility for maintaining it. And that's the choice Darius faced at the end of his terrible working lunch.

∼

"You know, as bad as things are in the world today, I would not want to have children if I were your age."

This veteran had violated her responsibility to a younger teacher, perfectly illustrating how damaging negativity can be to one person. Later on in his career, Darius would see plenty of examples of how negative talk like this could impact a hallway, a department, or an entire school.

Being a captive audience of one, Darius was happy that lunch was ending. But more than just getting away, he couldn't let her negativity have the last word. After all, he was in jeopardy of sitting next to Karen for the afternoon session. His response was perfect, in its timing and its clarity.

Darius looked Karen in the eye, smiled, and replied. "I can't wait."

For once, she was speechless.

May we all make the best effort to confront negatives and negativity in a way that benefits our students, our colleagues, and the families in our school community as professionals.

Taking responsibility for our morale is the final piece in the puzzle of defining professionalism and serves as the final step we must take to build trust within our school communities.

CHAPTER 9

Conclusions

We've gone to great lengths to spell out the rigors of the job, the steps to improvement, and the legal obligations related to serving *in loco parentis*. By now, you've probably figured it out. More than a plan of organization, a set of steps to follow, or a manifesto of personal beliefs; professionalism is, at its core, an attitude of self-discipline and service. A dedication to building relationships, and building capacity within our ranks.

But by their nature, attitudes can be fickle. Put one hundred different people to work in a school and you'll have one hundred attitudes, often at convergence with each other, in play. Employing the TRUST framework described in this book is how we normalize the high bar of service we want to meet as we interact daily in our school communities. When educators commit to this type of attitude and conduct, we can draw some very important conclusions.

The Value of the TRUST Framework

Let's step outside the field of education for a moment. When you consider the needs of customers, students, patients, and the general public, the more you realize that the TRUST framework travels well across all career fields.

Ask a business owner what they're looking for in a young, new hire, and the last thing you'll hear is the actual skills done on the job. That's the training they provide. A contractor, desperate to hire qualified high school graduates, described it this way, *"We're looking for people who can come to work on time, pass a drug test, and read a tape measure."*

He wants what every business or organization wants: job candidates who are employable. Then, as he began to describe the constant mishaps committed by the younger generation of workers in the areas of customer service, personal etiquette, and hospitality, I stopped him and offered a better description:

"You mean professionalism, right?"

He quickly nodded in agreement.

That's what the TRUST framework provides. Change out the word "educator" in the previous eight chapters for any other career, and the effect is the same. Dedication to purpose, a focus on safety, communication (including listening) skills, the ability to employ self-discipline, and a positive attitude. Take those skills into any job interview, and more often than not, you come away successful. If trust is present, the other details sort themselves out.

Later on, as that contractor explained the income that a high school graduate can earn in the construction field by age 25—easily reaching into the six-digits—I quickly realized that dedication, service, and work ethic are as important to students as our curriculum.

When employers ask for graduates who can simply focus on the importance of their job, and serving others, this is enough confirmation that the TRUST framework, which provides common ground between stakeholders in any field, translates well into business and industry.

The current work environment serves as an opportunity for educators to model the value of building trust within our communities. Call it family, teamwork, or whatever you like, but children will learn more when they are in the care of educators who focus on the most important things.

The TRUST framework for professional conduct provides a scaffold that supports educators as they serve the school community, and model the qualities students so desperately need to be successful when they move on after graduation. It turns professionalism, which often resembles an unattainable and undefined mirage, into an achievable goal.

Professionalism is a Moving Target

Change, just like personal attitudes, is a force to be reckoned with, and will always factor into decisions about acceptable educator conduct. But opinions on professionalism will always come from the eye of the beholder. As a child of the 1980's with two educator-parents in rural North Mississippi, my personal preferences about professional educator conduct might be a bit different from that of a teacher from Los Angeles, California, who was born after the year 2000 and raised by immigrant parents.

The first and most important question regarding the definition for professional conduct in a school community is, "Who gets to make the decision?"

The trends that change our society will always factor into expectations for educator conduct. How a school spells out that conduct should be a process. A great example is a perennial hot-button topic on educator professionalism: Jeans days. Does wearing blue jeans at work constitute a breakdown in professional conduct? It certainly generates a lot of conversation. Let's look at it through our framework of TRUST.

+ Can teachers carry out all their duties related to teaching and learning while wearing blue jeans at school?
  YES.

- Can teachers remain vigilant to safety concerns while wearing blue jeans at school?
  YES.
- Can teachers communicate effectively with all parties in the school community while wearing blue jeans at school?
  YES.
- Can teachers maintain the appropriate decision making, relational, and mental balance necessary to their work while wearing blue jeans at school?
  YES.
- Can teachers sustain a high personal morale while wearing blue jeans at school?
  YES.

That's a unanimous YES to all five of the TRUST factors of professional conduct. Case closed, right?

Not so fast.

You wouldn't pay a swim instructor to wear blue jeans and stand on the side of the pool as she watches your Kindergartener flail around in the shallow end. And I'm guessing you'd have a difficult time eating one of those wonderful burritos from Chipotle if the requisite gloves weren't worn by the kid who made it. Professional dress should fit the professional work.

Applying professional dress into the TRUST framework of educator conduct is a wonderful culture building conversation for teachers and administrators to have. Can teachers do their jobs in any kind of clothing? Well, not really. But it's important to point out that professional dress, or any other type of professional conduct, isn't just a decision to be outsourced to the beholder. It should also be appropriate to the job. Which brings us back to attitude.

I've seen teachers who wear jeans more than their staff dress code allows, who routinely push their students to extremely high levels of achievement. And I've also seen teachers who wore a necktie to work every day in a classroom that was absolute bedlam. A three-piece suit, a dress, or blue jeans won't make or break the professional conduct of an educator. A bad attitude will.

An important point to remember in the back-and-forth on jeans days is that denim is a fashion trend. Perhaps a more important question to answer in establishing professional dress codes, is: Where are the trends heading?

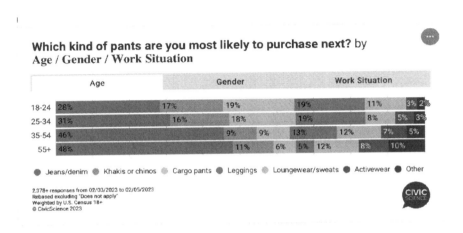

Which kind of pants are you most likely to purchase next? by Age / Gender / Work Situation

	Age		Gender		Work Situation			
18-24	28%	17%	19%	19%	11%		3%	2%
25-34	31%	16%	18%	19%	8%		5%	3%
35-54	46%	9%	9%	13%	12%	7%	5%	
55+	48%	11%	6%	5%	12%	8%	10%	

● Jeans/denim ● Khakis or chinos ◉ Cargo pants ● Leggings ◉ Loungewear/sweats ● Activewear ● Other

2,378+ responses from 02/03/2023 to 02/05/2023
Rebased excluding 'Does not apply'
Weighted by U.S. Census '18+
© CivicScience 2023

CIVIC SCIENCE

Civic Science (2023), a branch of Carnegie Mellon University, asked that question. Notice the breakdown of which types of pants each age group plans to purchase next. If this trend continues, the conversation in a few years will transition to the appropriateness of Leggings Day instead of Jeans Day.

My point? Well, I guess it's that fashion trends are…trendy. And, that the debate over jeans days really isn't the issue. The conversation around jeans is just an extension of the complex question we contemplated at the outset of this discussion: "*What is professionalism?*"

Go back to that checklist of questions about jeans days and substitute any issue into it. Then discuss it with the team. That's always a better gauge of professional conduct than the conventional wisdom.

You want to allow jeans as professional dress? Fine. You want to ban them? Fine. But regardless of your school's choice, the policy shouldn't start without first having a conversation about educator conduct and attitude.

And if jeans days have become such a point of contention, step back and think about the bigger picture for a moment. If a topic like wearing blue jeans at school can generate such angst, and cries out for input from all stakeholders, then how could the TRUST framework impact a faculty-level conversation on the best mode of communication for changes to the school calendar, a school-level policy for accepting (or not accepting) late work, or a school's cell phone policy? Viewing these issues through the lens of building TRUST offers a wonderful opportunity to introduce some inclusive leadership up and down the ranks, and give more teachers a voice in building a stronger culture.

If the goal is to build trust within our school community, then considerations about appearance absolutely matter. Fair or not, our community will make a judgment about us by what they see. And don't forget, we do the same thing when we walk into a bank, or roll up to a drive-thru window.

Before we jump headfirst into a de facto "uniform" for teachers that always includes denim, we should also consider what our professional dress says about our attitude toward the job. If we are going to decry the perceived lowering of the status of educators in society's eye, we can't also contribute to that perception by coming to work with a sloppy appearance, or in dress that communicates a poor attitude toward our work. (Biaggini, 2003)

And keeping up public appearances isn't even our greatest concern here. Never forget, what is caught is equally important as what is taught. Our students (you can read that word as future educators) will shape their attitudes towards school from ours. How's that for a scary thought? It's important to give them a good picture of our attitude every day. As trends change, we would do well to prevent one generation of educators, who happen to be in charge at a given moment in time, from becoming the deciding factor on professional conduct.

Trends will change. The fashion industry ensures it so they can turn a profit. A better use of our time would be a conversation within schools about what constitutes professional attitude, dress, conduct, efficient modes of communication, etc., with the understanding that

> **Our students will shape their attitudes towards school from ours.**

over time, ideas about professionalism will change as well. We must be able to adjust. The TRUST framework offers a path toward accepting that change in a way that benefits our students, their families, and our colleagues.

Mentorship is an Underrated Aspect of Professionalism

We've already discussed how the village plays a role in raising children. That idea translates well into our field. But when you consider the induction of new educators into the profession, no analogy could be more appropriate.

It most definitely takes a village to raise an educator. We don't discuss mentorship nearly enough among our ranks.

Professionalism, provided through our framework of building TRUST, depends on a deep commitment to our colleagues. But collaboration, a group effort to reflect on practice and improve together, isn't the only aspect of that commitment. Trusting a colleague implies a deeper responsibility than just meeting regularly to look at data.

Mentoring young educators is the embodiment of our calling. Think back to the beginning of your career. One of your first memories

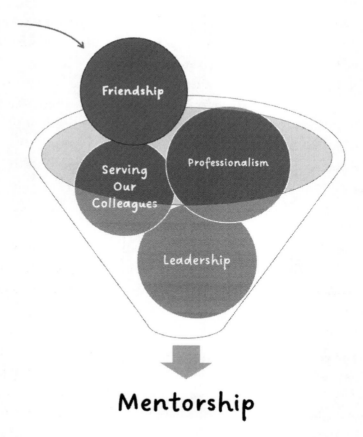

Mentorship

is undoubtedly the veterans who functioned as life savers, telling you what to expect in that first conference, how to handle a tough student, or explaining why the principal made the comments that bothered you. Their backgrounds are as varied as our class rosters, but the common theme among them all is a willingness to serve.

We've mentioned the phrase, "Everyone is a leader" often in our discussion on professionalism. Mentorship also fits that idea perfectly. Having grown up with two educators for parents, I was fortunate to learn this lesson early. In addition to their wisdom, the entire staff at their school served as a ready-made field of mentors who pushed, pulled, and led me to where I am today. One situation from my senior football season illustrates that support network. That season was notable for its moral victories.

Morton had a strong team that year, with a college prospect at running back. As I warmed up on the sideline, Dr. John Perry walked by on his way to the bleachers. Dr. Perry was a former principal who had come out of retirement to teach physics. Walking to his seat, he threw me a classic science-teacher quote. *"Hope the velocity on those passes exceeds the speed of your defenders tonight!"*

We took a 9 – 7 lead just before halftime when one of those passes connected. It was a textbook Hail Mary. I released it as I was knocked into the opposing bench. When I heard the cheers of our home crowd, I realized my friend Jesse Sawyer had hauled it in forty yards downfield for a touchdown. Unfortunately, none of my passes in the second half received any providential blessings. We lost the game 24 – 9.

On Monday morning, we again talked about velocity in physics class. When my headache became a topic of discussion, Dr. Perry asked a few probing questions, and I learned that the flash I saw at the end of a rather rough quarterback sack on Friday was likely a concussion. The lesson quickly transitioned to the force applied by the Panthers' defensive tackle to my helmet, which dug several inches into the turf.

The lesson continued the following morning. Dr. Perry found me before school and took me to the biology lab. A blood pressure cuff and stethoscope appeared. He checked my vital signs and we quickly found my dad to discuss those headaches. I was in a doctor's office before lunch. To my knowledge, Dr. Perry never received any official medical training. But if he'd offered some advice that day, I would have gladly taken it. His dedication led to that kind of influence.

Behind his big persona, we knew Dr. Perry cared. Years later, I was blessed by another servant mentor who also illustrated this caring service. Dr. Gerald Hasselman taught my first graduate level leadership class, *The Basics of Leadership*. Two decades later, the class continues.

Seven years after completing that degree in administration, when I learned I would interview for an assistant principal position, Dr. Hasselman was my first call. I scribbled down more notes during that phone call than I ever took in his classroom. Thanks to his coaching, I got the job.

Leadership is a hot topic today because conventional wisdom says we are in a drought when it comes to finding stellar leaders in our society. Walking around all day with our heads in our phones, we believe the algorithms over our own eyes. Social media throws athletes, entertainers, and politicians at us as society's best examples. But these attention-grabbers rarely live up to the title on their pedestal. Service is a foreign concept to them, so leadership and mentorship are, too.

Meanwhile, we rub elbows every day with dozens of servant leader mentors as we grow up, or start a new job. They are tough on us, they push us. They aren't afraid to tell us the truth about ourselves when we need to hear it. They hold us to a professional standard and make us better. We wouldn't have survived those first few years in the classroom without them.

Dr. Perry and Dr. Hasselman received their Doctorates of Education decades ago. But their influence was far greater than any title they were ever given by a university, or some school board. They earned that authority the hard way, by leading people to success, and serving with their colleagues through difficult times...For decades.

Through their service, they shaped generations. Influence that powerful can only come from years of dedication to others, from someone who proves that they have our best interests at heart. That's the power of mentorship to our field.

∼

As we interact with new teachers, high on theorized certainty, low on experience, and shaken by rookie mistakes, we see ourselves. But memories from our first years don't always translate well into our relationships with new teachers.

"Look, kid. You'd better buckle up if you plan on letting them run over you like that now. Just wait until we get to February. It will be horrible, and will only get worse."

This is the type of tough self-talk we would use to critique ourselves if we could go back in time. But brutal honesty is usually just brutal. Comments like this aren't constructive, they're confrontational. Because they don't teach. Professionals welcome the newbies in and show them the way. If there is one thing we all have in common, it's that first year. And no matter how far removed from those first days we get, we can still replay those mistakes from year one in our heads. This fact makes mentorship tough for teachers, because it takes patience. When you've given so much of that precious quality to your students, it can be hard to spend quality time helping a struggling colleague late in the day.

Give the rookies time to explain their theories. And if they've been misled by some professor whose classroom experience is mostly imagined, explain why and help them understand potential consequences in the real world. It's OK to let them make some mistakes, too. After all, experience is the best teacher. But the view held by some that first-year educators need to "survive in the deep end because that's how I learned" is a recipe for failure.

Take these new educators under your wing. Teach them how to withstand the tough days and how to properly celebrate the good ones. Show them how respect from students is infinitely more valuable than popularity. Help them understand the importance of a structured classroom to kids who may have never seen structure, especially as the year starts. And help them know when they can eventually employ leniency so that it actually works. That's how we get stronger.

Like you, I benefited from dozens of these servant leaders. But take this final lesson on mentorship from me. Let those mentors know how much of an impact they made on you, before it's too late. I promise, you will be glad you did.

Tomorrow's Professionals are Sitting in Our Classrooms Now

When we view our colleagues as an extended family, we need to consider the long-term survival of our profession. That's our responsibility, too. School effectiveness isn't the only outcome of understanding professional conduct and building trust. Another major issue plaguing schools that we must address can be summarized in a single six-word phrase—because we do not hear it nearly enough:

"I want to be a teacher."

Perhaps it isn't spoken as much because of our fast-paced lifestyles. Maybe the world doesn't value serving others anymore. Popular culture has redefined leadership as serving yourself. Forget about the root causes of the problems, or taking responsibility for them. Instead, we've busied ourselves with other issues and taken our eye off the ball. As professionals, we have a responsibility to encourage, equip, and inspire young people to be tomorrow's educators.

Political leaders—from both sides—pay lip service to this idea. But they never fully commit. The typical teacher pay-raise cycle is a good example. Their constant focus on winning the political high ground looks like siblings bickering on the back seat. Then, after the last election is safely out of memory, it's back to business as usual. Meanwhile, this precious statement is still out there, waiting for someone serious to engage it.

Education interest groups drive the political infighting that stifles our cause. If you believe arguments from the right, teachers' unions are subversively pushing leftist ideals on our kids and encouraging teachers not to work. If you believe arguments from the left, conservatives are trying to blow up the system, send us back to the days of the one room schoolhouse, and set our society back a hundred years. Those who don't know which group to believe, namely students, end up disengaging from the process. Kids aren't interested in joining that fray.

Education bureaucrats welcome the sentiment. But then they smother it with testing requirements and red tape that only damage the trust educators place in their leaders. Some in this group are so far removed from the school, they'd need a telescope to see a classroom. Their rules and requirements, offered as "help," often end up restricting options and driving parents away.

Administrators share responsibility, too. They constantly hunt for good teaching candidates. But are they doing everything they can to grow the teachers in their building now? Retainment is the most valuable form of teacher recruitment. School leaders are often saddled with burdensome requirements to satisfy a bureaucrat or some legal rule. We can't let those regulations take priority over our students and teachers. Perhaps moving those items down the list and investing more time in relationship building would help.

And then there are the teachers on the front lines. They are constantly hoping for good students, but are they doing everything they can to grow every single kid in their classroom? Our ranks of current educators cry about pay, as though money is the only thing that matters to someone who answers a calling. Pay is important, but our calling implies so much more.

This phrase tells us someone is devoting their life to a higher purpose. It means we did our job with that kid. We didn't choose the job to get rich, we chose it to give. There are good people up and down the chain who positively impact kids on a daily basis. But an added danger is the constant blame being tossed up and down the ladder as one group indicts the other as being the weak link. There is enough blame to go around for everyone.

The stress and anxiety from dealing with egos and kid drama and attitudes and apathy can push us into a tunnel vision that passes up the importance of modeling mentorship and leadership. Don't ever forget one key feature of professionalism we haven't mentioned yet: it's OK for educators to have fun. If we ignore student relationships and camaraderie with our colleagues, or if we don't enjoy our work, kids can tell. What they see teachers doing, how they see teachers interacting, is a stronger message than any lecture. Constant negativity pushes our kids further away. Enjoyment and fulfillment are what they need to see. Regularly.

～

"I want to be a teacher." I said this phrase one time. And of all people, an educator immediately tried to talk me out of it. I'm afraid there are many educators today who also wouldn't encourage it. But how we deal with this short, simple, hope-inspiring phrase is the answer to the world's education problem.

Think about it. How would you respond if your own child, preparing to begin college, explained her career choice to you by saying, *I want to be a teacher?* Deep down in your heart, be honest. If your answer would be anything less than "Congratulations", then you, dear educator, need to think about why.

What can we do differently in our work so that the collective reaction to this statement improves? What can we do to restore teaching to that high place in society where it belongs? The answers to those deep questions are looking back at us in the mirror.

Commit to building trust. Commit to a high standard of professional conduct. The teacher shortage will never end until we inspire more young people to become educators. But we must live and work like we actually want to hear it. Educators, parents, politicians, communities. All of us.

It's an issue that is urgent, like school safety; and important, like competent instruction. That is our task, educators. Let's work together for a change.

Professional Conduct is a Personal Contribution to School Culture

Let's reflect. On a scale of 1 - 10, how would you rate your emphasis on instruction, attention to safety, communication, and morale at work? I bet your number was somewhere North of seven. Now, consider your school community. How would your coworkers rate you? This honest, introspective look at professional conduct is a good way to consider the strength, or weakness, of an educator's contribution to culture.

How would you rate the general attitude toward the work of educating students in your school? Before you spend too much time working your way down the roster, let's go back to the one person on campus that you can actually change. It only takes one educator to change a school. Focusing on the basics, maintaining a positive attitude, and prioritizing the most important aspects of our work will change you. And it will also affect your colleagues.

Professional conduct is an educator's personal contribution to building culture, which means a daily commitment to building TRUST within the school community. We do that by maintaining a constant focus on teaching and learning, safety, communication, balance, and morale.

Are you elevating your school's culture? Committing ourselves daily to the TRUST framework is how we ensure that contribution to our communities is always a positive one.

CHAPTER 10

An Unexpected
Rite of Passage

P*omp and Circumstance* starts to play, and the seniors march in. These young people have waited their entire lives for today. The class president nervously strides to the podium to welcome families into the school.

It's not graduation, though. It's Class Day, the final day of school, celebrated at many schools with an awards ceremony. Every spring, families gather at schools across America to commemorate thirteen years of hard work.

Two hours later, after the awards table is empty and all the bragging has ended, the crowd experiences one of the most underrated events of every school year held at many schools: The senior video. This amateur video collage is one of the corniest rites of passage associated with raising kids in America. It punctuates the group's final time together at school by celebrating all the moments kids remember. Pep rally costumes, formal wear at prom, standing-room-only in the student section, and candid snapshots from lunch, all set to the pop music of the day.

This conclusion to Senior Class Day certainly isn't the most academic function of the school year. But for all the accolades and

153

scholarships handed out, the senior video is the only item on the program that commands everyone's attention. For ten solid minutes, the entire crowd is mesmerized. They even put their cell phones down.

The video hits parents where it hurts. They lean forward at this unexpected look back in time. The senior video gives them one final glimpse of their soon-to-be-adult still being a kid.

But then, more memories flood in. Halloween carnivals, field trips to the aquarium, Dr. Seuss day. It's brutal. These folks just spent the morning celebrating their kids' journey through high school. But right there in the bleachers, shoulder-to-shoulder with somebody's weird uncle, the senior video shoves them further down the path. Tissues are out before the first song ends.

On the floor, the students aren't so reflective just yet. They're too busy having a ball. Mike's outfit at the powder puff game was a little too revealing. Kayla's shady look in the photobooth was an early sign of prom night drama. The pictures are hilarious. But as soon as everyone settles back in, Taylor Swift fades out. The moment gets heavy. Their confused looks betray their thoughts.

"What do we do now?"

Class is finally, officially, dismissed.

The Value of Self-Discipline

As important as the first day of kindergarten can be, this scene that plays out every spring in many gyms and auditoriums across America is even bigger. By the time parents fight through the trenches of adolescence and get blindsided by the teenage years, forcing them to reflect on it all in a sappy ten-minute video is just cruel. Parents watch their whole lives flash before their eyes, to the tune of *Blank Space*.

Our pledge is to partner with parents through this life change. This isn't possible if we aren't seen as worthy of standing in their place. And even if our personal beliefs don't line up directly with theirs, we can employ our training, expertise, and commitment to service—our *professionalism*—to be that partner. We are the common ground our country so desperately seeks.

> We are the common ground our country so desperately seeks.

One final illustration of the TRUST framework comes from another organization that depends heavily on trust, the United States Army. Lieutenant General Hal Moore, famed commander of the 7th U.S. Cavalry Regiment during the Vietnam War, understood the value of the professional routines within his unit. If you've ever seen the movie, *We Were Soldiers*, then you're familiar with his exploits.

General Moore was also a pioneer in the study of leadership. He explained the value of professional conduct to the men he led this way:

"A soldier's professional attitude towards his job; how he maintains his equipment, how he communicates, and how he carries himself at all times, is the difference between life or death." (Moore & Guardia, 2017, p.201)

General Moore wanted his soldiers to focus on maintaining equipment, staying disciplined in their daily work, and taking care of each other up and down the ranks. If they didn't, they were risking their lives. As educators, we don't deal with the same dangers, but taking a flippant attitude toward our speech or our responsibilities could harm students, and could cost us our livelihoods.

Ultimately, you and your coworkers will define professional conduct at your school by the sum of your actions. So, what is the comfort zone for conduct in your school? Is self-discipline valued? The day-to-day expectations and conversations that are ingrained into everyone's pattern of work explain where your group's priorities lie.

Is it uncomfortable to start conversations about improving some aspect of your work? Is there a level of comfort in speaking negatively about any and everything at school? How often is blame the first answer to a problem? As an individual, you can't be personally responsible for the professional expectations of the group, but you can most definitely do your part to elevate them.

Hopefully, you don't see yourself swimming upstream in that effort. And if you are fortunate enough to work in a healthy, supportive professional culture, a true professional learning community, congratulations. If that's the case, just buckle up and enjoy the ride. There is nothing so fulfilling as fitting into a team of educators who contribute together in this meaningful work.

This Is What's Right about Education in America

Back in the gym, those professionals watch kids and parents cross the finish line from a different perspective. They watch that goofy video, see the emotions on display, and laugh. Because sometimes that's the only way to keep from crying. Teachers hear the stories from home. They see the differences and still figure out how to teach and protect their students, with all their different strengths, weaknesses, and attitudes.

For all the talk about the rigors of this job, there are few career fields that offer the rewards that come with teaching and serving in a school. It's awe-inspiring to see the mission statement fulfilled, while surveying a crowd that illustrates the word "juxtaposition" better than any English teacher ever could. The ten-minute video helps educators complete another step of the school-calendar cycle, and offers them a rare chance to exhale and appreciate the moment.

Memories flood in for them, too. First, the high points. Light bulb moments when tough situations remind a person why they chose teaching as a career. Kayla's Monday after prom showed a level of maturity that few adults could muster. And reflecting on the big picture helps the low points fade a little. It turns out Ms. Pena's favorite student this year is the same scrawny kid she pulled out of a fight three years ago.

Then the music suddenly stops, and everyone awakens from their trance. The students look around, hoping to connect for one more laugh. Parents realize an adult is now standing before them. Teachers now step out of the trench for a moment and recognize these young people for what they've become, friends.

And for the kids, everything is different now. The lunch bell is suddenly void of any meaning. Even the toughest cases of senioritis have dried up by this point. At the best schools, everyone in the room—parents, students, and professionals—can reflect on another successful year together.

This is what's right about education in America. A community of people, led by the professionals, all pulling in the same direction, bound together by trust. And how

> "We did the best we could with them."

do we get there? Soft skills? Hardly. Service skills is a better description. Devoting a career to serving students and families is a beautiful picture of dedication, service, and trust. That's professionalism.

Godspeed, as you fulfill your calling to this great profession.

Acknowledgements

I guess we all have different reactions to the maddening occurrence of a canceled flight. But as my wife and I enjoyed a walk through the streets of Boston back on July 18, 2019, an email from Southwest Airlines set events in motion that led to the book you just read.

I had no idea at the time, but the next day was an important one for me. As we awaited an open seat on an unknown flight home, we found a quiet corner of Logan Airport at 6:00 in the morning. Then I opened my MacBook, and started typing.

The next day my blog, Personal Professional Development, had its first post. The ideas I started kicking around in that space filled many of the pages in this work. I guess I should be thankful to Southwest for providing the extra time to write.

When I completed my dissertation, I looked forward to writing the acknowledgements section with joy. That was the one page where I could actually write what I wanted to. But as I type today, I find myself terrified of this page. Twenty-four years as an educator, and five years of writing, makes a person keenly aware of the impact so many educators, family, and friends have on you. This section will be woefully inadequate to thank all the people who had a hand in my career, and subsequently, this work.

God has blessed me with a wonderful career as a teacher, coach, and administrator. Answering His call to this field has been a blessing that I cannot easily explain. All thanks go to Him for his blessings and guidance.

My wife, Amanda, and our children; Harrison, Marin, Brandt, and Leighton have fueled me through this new chapter in my career. Without their support, and even more patience, this work wouldn't exist. I love you all dearly.

The blog notwithstanding, I actually got my start as an education writer back in the 1990s. That's when my dad paid me $1 a page to type his handwritten grad school papers. Using a borrowed computer, I copied his thoughts on educational leadership gleaned from the likes of Barth and Marzano. But the bigger lesson was watching my dad serve as a principal, and my mom as an English teacher, and seeing the rock-solid service they provided to our community for decades. When I think of my mentors, I think of Dwight and Judy Lollar first. Thank you!

The team of professionals who inspired me to write, and helped edit this book. Wesley Quick, Syl Burrell, and Brent Brownlee embody trust. I will forever be thankful for their influence on me. You may know educators who carry the banner well for their schools and colleagues. These three teammates of mine exceeded that effort. At times, they carried me. Serving on a team with them has been one of the highest points in a charmed career for me.

In addition to their support, I also received help from several other colleagues. Christy Walker, Jamie Dickson, Wesly Bolden, and Clay Norton offered insight that aided my efforts to define educator professionalism.

And then there is the gentleman who led to this work's publication. I met Jimmy Casas after conducting a book study on *Culturize* years ago. The field of education may not have a stronger ambassador in its ranks today. Jimmy's understanding of school culture, and his gift of motivation, have served as a specific inspiration for me. Working with him, Jeff Zoul, Kheila Casas, and the team at ConnectEDD Publishing to define educator professionalism and detail the way our schools can rebuild trust within their communities has been a joy. Thank you!

Nason Lollar
April 25, 2024
Flora, Mississippi

References

Biaggini, J. (2003). What professionalism means for teachers today. *Education Review, 18*(2), 5-11.

Casas, J. (2017). *Culturize: Every Student. Every Day. Whatever It Takes.* Dave Burgess Consulting, Inc.

Commisso, D. (2023, February 6). Jeans are getting faded out by Gen Z shoppers and remote workers. *Civic Science.* https://civicscience.com/jeans-are-getting-faded-out-by-gen-z-shoppers-and-remote-workers

Covey, S. (1989). *The seven habits of highly successful people.* Simon & Schuster.

Darling-Hammond, S., et al. (2023). The dynamic nature of student discipline and discipline disparities. *Proceedings of the National Academy of Sciences, 120*(17), 1-10. https://doi.org/10.1073/pnas.2118204120

DuFour, R., & Marzano, R. (2011). *Leaders of learning.* Solution Tree Press.

Elmore, R. (2000). *Building a new structure for school leadership.* The Albert Shanker Institute.

Eisenhower, D. (1954, August 19). Address at the second assembly of the World Council of Churches. Evanston, Illinois.

Kafele, B. (2019). *Is my school a better school because I lead it?* ASCD.

Kafele, B. (2021). *The equity & social justice education 50: Critical questions for improving opportunities and outcomes for Black students.* ASCD.

Love, N., Stiles, K., & Mundry, S. (2008). *The data coach's guide to improving learning for all students: Unleashing the power of collaborative inquiry.* Corwin Press.

Mead, M. (1928). *Coming of age in Samoa: A psychological study of primitive youth for western civilization.* William Morrow & Co.

Moore, H., & Guardia, M. (2017). *Hal Moore on leadership: Winning when out-gunned and outmanned.* CreateSpace Independent Publishing Platform.

National Center on Education Statistics. (2021). *Report on indicators on school crime and safety: 2021.* U.S. Department of Education. https://nces.ed.gov/programs/crimeindicators/index.asp

National Center on Education Statistics. (2018). *The condition of education, 2018: Characteristics of public school teachers who completed alternative route to certification programs.* U.S. Department of Education. https://nces.ed.gov/pubsearch/pubsinfo.asp?pubid=2018144

Rogers, C., & Farson, R. (1957). *Active listening.* Industrial Relations Center of the University of Chicago.

The Holy Bible. (2002). *New International Version.* Zondervan.

Yeager, D., et al. (2013). Breaking the cycle of mistrust: Wise interventions to provide critical feedback across the racial divide. *Journal of Experimental Psychology: General, 143*(2), 804-824. https://doi.org/10.1037/a0033906

About the Author

Having served twenty-four years in the field of education, Dr. Nason Lollar has leveraged those experiences into his first book, *The Five Principles of Educator Professionalism*.

Nason began his career in the classroom, serving as a high school math and social studies teacher, and as a baseball coach for fourteen years. He then transitioned to administration, serving as a high school assistant principal for nine years. He currently serves as a lead principal.

His journey as a student of Educational Leadership began with graduate work at Mississippi College, and culminated with a Doctorate of Education from William Carey University in 2018. In 2023, Nason was honored by the Mississippi Association of Secondary School Principals as state Assistant Principal of the Year.

Connect with Nason: On X, @nasonlollar, through his Facebook page, *Personal Development*, or on his blog, nasonlollar.wordpress.com.

More from ConnectEDD Publishing

Since 2015, ConnectEDD has worked to transform education by empowering educators to become better-equipped to teach, learn, and lead. What started as a small company designed to provide professional learning events for educators has grown to include a variety of services to help educators and administrators address essential challenges. ConnectEDD offers instructional and leadership coaching, professional development workshops focusing on a variety of educational topics, a roster of nationally recognized educator associates who possess hands-on knowledge and experience, educational conferences custom-designed to meet the specific needs of schools, districts, and state/national organizations, and ongoing, personalized support, both virtually and onsite. In 2020, ConnectEDD expanded to include publishing services designed to provide busy educators with books and resources consisting of practical information on a wide variety of teaching, learning, and leadership topics. Please visit us online at connecteddpublishing.com or contact us at: info@connecteddpublishing.com

Recent Publications:

Live Your Excellence: Action Guide by Jimmy Casas

Culturize: Action Guide by Jimmy Casas

Daily Inspiration for Educators: Positive Thoughts for Every Day of the Year by Jimmy Casas

Eyes on Culture: Multiply Excellence in Your School by Emily Paschall

Pause. Breathe. Flourish. Living Your Best Life as an Educator by William D. Parker

L.E.A.R.N.E.R. Finding the True, Good, and Beautiful in Education by Marita Diffenbaugh

Educator Reflection Tips Volume II: Refining Our Practice by Jami Fowler-White

Handle With Care: Managing Difficult Situations in Schools with Dignity and Respect by Jimmy Casas and Joy Kelly

Disruptive Thinking: Preparing Learners for Their Future by Eric Sheninger

Permission to be Great: Increasing Engagement in Your School by Dan Butler

Daily Inspiration for Educators: Positive Thoughts for Every Day of the Year, Volume II by Jimmy Casas

The 6 Literacy Levers: Creating a Community of Readers by Brad Gustafson

The Educator's ATLAS: Your Roadmap to Engagement by Weston Kieschnick

In This Season: Words for the Heart by Todd Nesloney, LaNesha Tabb, Tanner Olson, and Alice Lee

Leading with a Humble Heart: A 40-Day Devotional for Leaders by Zac Bauermaster

Recalibrate the Culture: Our Why…Our Work…Our Values by Jimmy Casas

Creating Curious Classrooms: The Beauty of Questions by Emma Chiappetta

Crafting the Culture: 45 Reflections on What Matters Most by Joe Sanfelippo and Jeffrey Zoul

Improving School Mental Health: The Thriving School Community Solution by Charle Peck and Dr. Cameron Caswell

Building Authenticity: A Blueprint for the Leader Inside You by Todd Nesloney and Tyler Cook

Connecting Through Conversation: A Playbook for Talking with Kids by Erika Bare and Tiffany Burns

The Dream Factory: Designing a Purposeful Life by Mark Trumbo

Stories Behind Stances: Creating Empathy Through Hearing "The Other Side" by Chris Singleton

Happy Eyes: Becoming All Things to All People by Ryan Tillman

The Generative Age Artificial Intelligence and the Future of Education by Alana Winnick

Recalibrate the Culture: Action Guide by Jimmy Casas

Leading with PEOPLE: A Six Pillar Framework for Fruitful Leadership by Zac Bauermaster

A School Leader's Guide to Reclaiming Purpose by Frederick C. Buskey

Foundations of an Elite Culture: Building Success with High Standards and a Positive Environment by David Arencibia

Personalize: Meeting the Needs of All Learners by Eric Sheninger and Nicki Slaugh

Made in the USA
Coppell, TX
26 April 2025

48725111R00103